The Companies She Keeps

Tina Packer Builds A Theater

In memory of
Louis G. Cowan
(1909–1976)

The Companies She Keeps

Tina Packer Builds A Theater

Helen Epstein

Plunkett Lake Press   Cambridge, Massachusetts   1985

Also by Helen Epstein
CHILDREN OF THE HOLOCAUST

copyright © 1985 Helen Epstein

FIRST PRINTING 1985

Published by PLUNKETT LAKE PRESS
551 Franklin Street, Cambridge, Massachusetts 02139

All photographs used by permission of *Shakespeare & Company.*

Library of Congress Cataloging in Publication Data

Epstein, Helen, 1947–
  The companies she keeps.

  1. Packer, Tina, 1938–   . 2. Shakespeare & Company (Lenox, Mass.) 3. Theatrical producers and directors—United States—Biography. 4. Actors—Great Britain—Biography. I. Title.
PN2287.P2E67 1985   792′.0233′0924 [B]   85-6485
ISBN 0-9614696-0-9

Parts of this book were first published in the *Boston Review* and *Berkshire Magazine.*

Printed in the United States of America

Acknowledgments

During the summer of 1981, Kim Smedvig took me to The Mount in Lenox to see the correspondence between Edith Wharton and Henry James dramatized. Tina Packer was playing Edith. Dennis Krausnick was playing Henry. They were so good that, after the performance, I stayed behind to meet them and, for a few hours, we sat on Edith Wharton's pleasant terrace talking. They told me they had founded a Shakespeare Company but mostly we talked about ghosts— the ghosts of Edith and Henry and Teddy Wharton that they and other members of the company had encountered late at night in the old mansion. I listened and laughed and thought: these are the kind of people I would like to write about.

The strictures of contemporary cultural reporting made that all but impossible. I had been writing Sunday arts pieces for the *New York Times* for nearly eight years by then and I knew the requirements for an assignment: an artist had to be "important" in the eyes of the editors; he (for in my experience it had almost always been a man) almost always had an aggressive press agent; and it helped enormously if there was a birthday, anniversary of debut, opening of a show, publication of a book or big concert pending. These things, I would subsequently tell my journalism students at New York University, were considered "news pegs," and justified what some of my editors called "giving space" to some artists or events and not others.

Before I wrote *Children of the Holocaust,* I had "pitched" the idea of a magazine piece about children of Holocaust survivors to the *New York Times*. I had been told the subject was unimportant and not newsworthy. At the time, there was no organization of children of survivors, no stationary with an impressive letterhead to validate their existence and no expert ready to vouch for the fact that they constituted a group. I am myself a child of Holocaust survivors but, for my editors, my opinion was not enough. Half a year later, after *Time Magazine* ran a story about the findings of an Israeli psychiatrist visiting Stanford University Medical School regarding this group, I got a telephone call from the *Times* Magazine: would I write a piece?

I was sure I wouldn't get far pitching the idea of Tina Packer's Shakespeare company in the Berkshires to the *New York Times* in 1981. She was surely not "important" enough; she employed no famous actors; the scale on which she operated was small; she didn't even go to New York in the winter! The story I wanted to tell was not easy to pitch either: it was the story of how a woman had built a theater company, but it was also the story of several long friendships and the story of how one woman artist found another woman artist's home vital to her own work. It took place in England and Berkshire County, Massachusetts. It was too unusual, too difficult to package and, although I discussed the idea with several magazine editors, none were interested.

One of the encouraging things about being a writer in the United States is that there are lots of markets. Three years later, in the spring of 1984, I got a call from Nicholas Bromell, who was then editor of the *Boston Review*. Bromell had obtained a grant from the Rockefeller Foundation to commission a set of long pieces on the arts in America: was there anyone I was interested in writing about? I told him: Tina Packer. Were it not for Bromell and the Rockefeller Foundation, this book would not have been written.

Bromell got my name from Ann-Marie Cunningham who, along with Margo Jefferson, Elizabeth Stone, Carol Sternhell, Ann Banks and myself formed a writer's group in New York several years ago. I thank them for their help and good company over the years. I miss their meetings and would miss them more were it not for my writing groups in Pittsfield (Barbara Coon, Linda Daube, Madeleine Hawboldt and Laurie Scace) and in Boston (Caryl Rivers, Bernice Buresh, Janet Robertson, Barbara Erlich White, Carolyn Toll, Sally Steinberg, Phyllis Karass, Diana Korzenik and Diane Cox) who heard parts of this book while I was writing it.

The research for this book was facilitated by the Ford Foundation, which permitted me use of its archives, by the generosity of members of *Shakespeare & Company,* and by Dick Kapp. Dean Richard A. Turner was instrumental in granting me a leave of absence from my job in New York University's Department of Journalism and I thank him for it.

I would also like to thank my friends Pamela Hollie, Karen Ryker, Gail Merrifield and Robin Miller for reading the manuscript and catching errors; Bernice Buresh volunteered to copy-edit; Margo Jefferson and Susan Mead, to proofread. I thank them and, most of all, I thank my husband for first thinking that this story would make a good book.

Helen Epstein
Cambridge, MA
March 15, 1985

On a fall evening in 1972, a rosy-faced English-woman in an enormous ankle-length orange tent dress turned up at Kristin Linklater's apartment in New York City's East Village. Eyes twinkling, she delivered greetings from various theater people in London along with her own irreverent appraisal of their activities. The two women chatted and traded theater gossip until the visitor came to the point of her visit: she said she was starting an international Shakespeare company that would marry young American actors and classical British training. She asked for Linklater's help.

Kristin Linklater had become accustomed to people seeking her out. A dark-eyed, contained, articulate woman born and raised in Scotland, she had trained as an actress and voice teacher in London but, like many Britons during the early 1960s, had decided that America was the place to be. She had come to New York in 1963 and had been hired at the Lincoln Center's brand-new repertory theater on the day after her arrival. She was internationally known for her "Linklater Technique," a method of training the actor's voice for performance, and she had taught and coached on Broadway as well as in the American regional theaters. She had received several foundation grants and had acquired a reputation for being canny and fierce. It was with a skepticism that was partly innate, partly the result of nine years in New York that she regarded this new arrival from Britain, this Tina Packer.

Tina Packer was then 34 years old, two years younger than Linklater, and had impressive credentials. She had trained as an actress at London's Royal Academy of Dramatic Arts, had worked as an Associate Artist with the Royal Shakespeare Company, and had appeared on various television serials for the BBC. But she had put all that behind her, she told Linklater. She wanted to direct, not act.

Linklater was not sure what to make of her. Packer was an outgoing soul. She giggled. She did not seem concerned about looking or acting important. She beamed out a friendliness and a kind of cheery pragmatism that seemed more American than English. She wore no make-up and her short brown hair looked as though she had cut it herself. She had a beguiling way of talking that charmed Linklater. When she paused between thoughts, her head tilted to one side and she looked like a chipmunk surprised in the woods. In her long orange Laura Ashley dress she might easily have been mistaken for a hippie from Tompkins Square Park across the street. But Packer was methodical in her queries of Linklater. She seemed impervious to the fact that she was in a new country, where she had no network of contacts, no friends, no name. She seemed to believe that she would found a Shakespeare company where she would produce and direct plays her own way. And she seemed to believe that she would fly back to London the following week-end with a Ford Foundation grant in her pocket to enable her to do just that.

Kristin Linklater listened with a courtesy that was as deep as her skepticism. "I didn't know if she was any good," she said years later. "She didn't seem young but she had a kind of ignorance about the basic facts of economic life. To come from London and think you could just tap into American riches was a pretty British idea at the time. I told her that *I* had had to work very hard. In order to get a grant, you had to have a track record. I told her she needed to have directed some shows over here. She needed to have a proper *visa*! She had a visitor's visa at the time! I imagine I said: you have a lovely idea, this international Shakespeare company, but it's just not going to work."

Linklater enumerated the many obstacles that stood between British directors and American money. She told Packer it was all fine and well that she had managed to see a programming officer at the Ford Foundation but that the important person there was MacNeil Lowry who rarely saw obscure strangers face to face. But Tina Packer had intrigued her. Linklater was struck by her energy, her intelligence, and perhaps most of all, by her drive. She gave the optimistic Englishwoman the names of some people who might help her obtain grant money. She also agreed, in the unlikely event that a company was formed, to serve as one of the British master teachers in it.

The two women said their good-byes. Tina Packer returned to London. Kristin Linklater, who actually *had* in her pocket $10,000 from the Ford Foundation, also left New York to work on a book. She was in residence at the Rockefeller Foundation's Villa Serbelloni in Italy, writing *Freeing the Natural Voice* (which has since become a classic text on voice production for actors) when she got an urgent message from Tina Packer. Packer had been awarded $132,000 from the Ford Foundation "to explore the roots of Elizabethan theater" with an Anglo-American company of actors and teachers. Would Linklater be able to join her in Alcester, just outside Stratford-upon-Avon in February of 1973?

10

Kristin Linklater said yes, as scores of other people would subsequently find themselves doing when Tina Packer asked them for their time, their money, or their ideas. Eventually, she became Director of Training in the enterprise of which Packer was Artistic Director. During the 1970s, they would criss-cross the Atlantic, working together in a variety of ways; 1978 would find them living communally in a decrepit mansion in the Berkshire Hills of Massachusetts; 1985 would see them settled in country houses heated by wood stoves.

By that time, Tina Packer would be director of not one but two Shakespeare companies—one on either end of the state of Massachusetts. In 1985, *Shakespeare & Company,* based in Berkshire County just outside Lenox, was planning its eighth season on a budget of $1.2 million and operating out of offices that once housed the servants of American novelist Edith Wharton. The *Boston Shakespeare Company,* based in the Musicians Mutual Relief Society Building in the center of Boston's renovated South End, had cancelled its eleventh season in order to avert bankruptcy and to build a sound financial base.

Twelve years after Tina Packer first outlined her plan to direct Shakespeare in Kristin Linklater's living room, many of its parts were in place. She had an inter-racial group of young North American actors working with a core of faithful and impressive British teachers. She had a summer stage in the resort area of the Berkshires and a winter stage in Boston. She had, for the past three years, taken her company to New York City where *Shakespeare & Company* had performed under the aegis of Joseph Papp, and she had gone on tour with the troupe to more than a dozen states.

Her plan was extraordinarily ambitious. For years people had been calling for the establishment of an American national repertory theater and for years American theater executives had said it could not be done: it was too expensive, the country was too large, there was no tradition of government subsidy, and no incentive for American actors to stick with one group. How could you keep talented actors with a repertory company when they would have to pass up movie and television opportunities for six months or a year? How could you pay them? The problems were insurmountable. Some American directors had tried to form such companies and had failed. Others thought it was not even worth trying.

Tina Packer would not be deterred. What she wanted was a year-round, classically-trained repertory group based on the English model but with an energy and emotional truth that she saw as distinctly American. She wanted to build what would be regarded as an American peer of the Royal Shakespeare Company in England.

Christina Packer was born September 28, 1938 in Wolverhampton, England, to parents who belonged, as she puts it, to "the risen working class." One of her grandmothers worked as a laundress, the other as a housemaid. Education financed by the state of England was her family's ticket up the social ladder. Her father became a probation officer who retired, at the age of 52, to write. Her mother taught school.

Packer describes them as liberal, permissive parents who taught their children ethics but instilled in them a dislike for organized religion, who ate a vegetarian diet, loved literature and the theater, and "encouraged their children's eccentricities." Packer's older sister, whom she remembers as "always outstanding," left England to make artificial limbs in a leper colony in Africa. Her two younger brothers became school teachers.

Wolverhampton was bombed during the war as was nearby Birmingham, and the Packer children were evacuated to a farm. After the war, the family moved to Nottingham, a small city which some English people living in America say is not unlike Boston. It had a large university, a polytechnic institute, several light industries (including hosiery, lace and bicycles) and a good repertory theater—as well as a treasury of folklore surrounding the figures of local sons D. H. Lawrence and Robin Hood.

After attending the local school in the shadow of her older sister, Tina was sent away to a Quaker boarding school where, her parents felt, she would develop more on her own, and where she would be taught in an atmosphere tolerant of difference. It was there that she first memorized set speeches from Shakespeare, as was the practice in most English secondary schools, and acted in plays. "I still remember acting out the death of Caesar and one of the boys on the floor trying to look up the English mistress's skirt," she recounted later, with one of her frequent chuckles. "Stabbing your fellow pupils—actually pushing a play knife in—is a hell of a lot more fun than sitting behind your desk reading *et tu Brute*. I didn't particularly enjoy just reading it."

The proximity of Stratford-upon-Avon made seeing Shakespeare easy and, during high shool, Tina Packer saw *The Merchant of Venice* and *The Taming of the Shrew* and *Twelfth Night* there.. She remembers those trips as major events of her adolescence: "Not just the plays themselves but the whole thing. Getting on the bus. The chatter. The trip to Stratford. Walking into the theater. The whole excitement of the adult world. Watching people perform in this ritualized fashion. Coming back on the bus at night. It was the heightened awareness that I liked."

Although her family regularly attended the repertory theater in Nottingham, no one thought about theater as a career and, for a time, Tina restricted her play-acting to making faces in the bathroom mirror. She belonged to the drama society at her school but was interested less in reading the plays than in arranging for backstage tours at Stratford during which she could meet the actors. Her father's wish to be a writer colored her own ambitions. She thought she would

14

Tina Packer at age eight

go to university, read English and become a writer herself. At the age of 16, she successfully wrote ten "O-level" examinations, the first required tests for university entrance in England but, two years later, while preparing her "A-levels" she began "wilting on the academic vine." She found she could not bear the time she spent sitting in classrooms. Her only interests were boys and the theater. She had been reading Hemingway's novels of American expatriate life in Europe and, as soon as her last A-level exam was over, she went to Paris for what was supposed to be a week with her older sister and a girlfriend.

It was 1956. A second generation of Americans was in Paris. With the clearsighted, straightforward determination that would later characterize her creation of a theater, Packer now set forth to meet and captivate a painter in Paris. During that week, she found what she was looking for. The man she chose was a thrice-married, 35-year-old American artist with precisely the kind of life and friends the 18-year-old somewhat provincial English girl had read about. Her older sister and girlfriend returned to England without her. For most of two years, Tina Packer moved with her painter from Montparnasse, in Paris, to a chateau in the Loire Valley, to the island of Majorca. She lived the way characters did in the Hemingway novels she had read: she ate garlic sausage, peasant bread, and drank red wine; she met disaffected intellectuals and artists and poets such as John Ashbery and Robert Graves. She stayed up talking about life and art till dawn, discussing the three novels that she began and then discarded after getting as far as "Chapter Three." During those two years, she met men and women who were, in effect, renegades in their countries of origin. They held fast to their own ideas and took pride in their independence. Some of these people became both models and mentors for Packer for the rest of her life.

16

Living with real writers made her understand that writing was not what she herself wished to do. At the back of her mind all the time she lived in France was that she wanted to become an actress. But his image conflicted with the way Packer had seen herself when she first met her American painter in a Paris cafe. "My idea of an actress then was someone like Diana Dors, unbuttoned on Page Three of the *Sun*," she later said. "I was used to serious artists by that time. I thought actors were frivolous people most unlike myself who was a serious Bohemian."

When she was twenty, the painter left her and Tina Packer returned—heart broken, she recalled with a sympathetic chuckle—to England. Returning to Nottingham after her two years abroad was out of the question. She settled in London where, for a while, she worked as a receptionist for a posh Knightsbridge chiropodist. This bored her so intensely that she talked her way into a staff position on a large women's magazine where colleagues later wrote about her "nibbled-off hair, bird-bright eyes, and black-stockinged legs." To recover from her first major love affair, Packer began attending London's theaters almost every night and up to three times on Saturdays when shows were scheduled for two, five, and eight. Despite her two-year immersion in the world of visual artists, theater had remained for her the form in which she found solace, as well as "a kind of ecstasy" and "a heightened sense of life." She would walk into theaters feeling depressed and lifeless, and walk out feeling fine. She saw *The Hostage* by Brendan Behan no fewer than ten times; she went to see Shelagh Delaney's *A Taste of Honey* seven times. The urge to get up on stage and perform grew stronger and stronger. After a few months of writing true-life stories and teen-age pieces for *Woman* magazine, she began to audition at London's drama schools. Her first attempts were unsuccessful but after half a year, she was accepted at the

18

Royal Academy of Dramatic Arts. Only about 20 people were accepted at RADA each year from well over 500 applicants. It was her second try.

Tina Packer had trouble during her first year at the school. She did not naturally take to the regimen of classes and, as she remembers it, even then, in 1962, RADA was becoming something of a closed circle. Her most successful classmates, she thought, were university men like Terry Hands (who later became a co-director of the Royal Shakespeare Company) or women whom she found "incredibly pretty." Some of them had acted extensively or had even directed plays at their university drama societies. She felt alternately inferior and superior to them. On the one hand, she had flunked her A-levels. On the other, she had been exposed to the best expatriate minds during her years in France. On one hand, she was not the classical prototype of a young ingenue—her features were too lively and quizzical, her manner too expansive, her body too round. On the other, she had, after all, *lived* a passionate love affair unlike her more parochial classmates. Even at 21, Packer had a strong impact on people, which was a quality that her drama school directors found more appropriate for character actresses than for leads. Also at issue for the first time in her life was the way she spoke English.

According to Packer, there was pressure at RADA for women to "speak well," a euphemism for speaking what was called BBC English, Standard English, Oxford English or South Kensington English. She spoke Nottingham. The English encouraged at RADA "shows you're part of the upper classes," Packer later told interviewers, "and it has occurred in England only over the last 100 years. It began when George III came to the throne with a German accent and members of his court began to say *baahhth* and other things like that to make him feel at home. That happened a long time after

Shakespeare who, by the way, spoke with a Warwickshire accent. It clearly had nothing to do with the Elizabethans.

"There's no point in eradicating your own accent: it's part of who you are. The idea is to lend what you have to the demands of Shakespeare. By the time I was at RADA, men no longer had to have standard accents because the new working class plays being written at the time had made stars of actors like Albert Finney, who talked Manchester. But women were still expected to push their voices to the front of their mouths and make plummy sounds. I worked with bone props—small pieces of bone that hold your mouth open while you learn to make pear-shaped vowels."

The training at RADA included elocution, during which veteran actresses taught Packer traditional delivery of Shakespearean lines. There was mime work, mask work, text work and period movement, which Packer found useful "but somewhat inhibiting if you haven't yet learned who you yourself are.

"What they do is expose you to an extraordinary range of plays, get you to stand up straight, and speak so that you can be heard at all times. The English actors who do best with that sort of training are the ones who are seething with inner life and who get from this training some sense of form. Those who aren't naturally vibrant have a hard time getting their inner life out."

The latter was not ever Packer's problem. She loved throwing herself about the stage so much that one of her teachers told her that she moved like a "spastic duck." Because of her energy and exuberance, other teachers suggested that she do Restoration comedy ("I had large bosoms and, you know, most Restoration comedy is *about* bosoms!") or working class, contemporary plays. She took badly to their suggestions because she was sure that she wanted to play Shakespeare and that her ideas about doing it were better

20

Receiving Ronson Award from Richard Attenburgh

than those of her teachers. At the same time, she did not have the confidence of her perceptions; she wanted her teachers to validate them. The roles she most wished to play were women who killed or were killed: Lady MacBeth, Cleopatra. Her teachers discouraged her when she told them this. Some said politely, "This is, of course, beyond your range." Others simply said, "No."

There is, oddly enough, no evidence of Packer's struggles at RADA anywhere but in her own published remarks. On the contrary, she graduated the drama school in 1964 with the Ronson Award for Most Promising Actress (which she accepted, according to the *Nottingham Evening Post and News,* with the words: "It's nice to win a cup or medal but cash at this moment is just what I need.")

In fact, she needed the money less than most of her class-mates. Packer had been on scholarship during her entire training at RADA and went straight to work after gradu-ating. She was a working actress at a time when half the estimated eleven thousand members of British Actors Equity were out of work on any given day of the week.

The role which Packer felt "turned things around" at drama school and won her the Ronson Award was that of Hilde Wangel in Henrik Ibsen's *The Master Builder.* While Hilde was not the heroine for women that Nora in *A Doll's House* became, she was, at least, a woman that Packer felt as some part of herself. Packer was reviewed as "gloriously alive, a genuinely fresh draught of air" by one paper and as "se-ductive, destructive, and skittish as the mood changed," by

the *London Times*. She went straight from school into playing repertory theater at Worthing.

By that time, she had been married for three years to Laurie Asprey, a fellow actor and photographer whom she had wed during her first term at RADA.

Within six months of graduation, her agent had arranged for Packer to audition for Peter Hall at the Royal Shakespeare Company and, after "ten terrifying auditions" she was asked to sign a three-year contract as an Associate Artist. On her opening night, she replaced Julie Christie as Luciana in *The Comedy of Errors* and over the next year and a half, worked with such directors as John Schlesinger, Peter Hall, Trevor Nunn and John Barton, a former Cambridge don and disciple of the literary critic F. R. Leavis. Leavis had taught his students to thoroughly analyze a text and place it in its proper social context. Barton passed on to Packer what Leavis had taught him, spending hours examining the structure of Shakespeare's verse. She found herself far happier at the RSC, far more in tune with her directors, than she had been at school. She worked closely with such revered actors as Paul Scofield. She felt that every day she was "exposed to terrific philosophical ideas just by working constantly on Shakespeare." She felt her physical strength grow by performing every night and her confidence increase as she worked on new roles. She loved living in the town of Stratford just two hours away from London. The only part of her life that was not working was her marriage.

"I should hate to think Laurie would ever put me before his career," she was quoted as saying in the *Birmingham Mercury* at the end of May, 1965, when she was 26 and enjoying her first flush of success as an RSC actress. "I don't think he should expect me to put him first. I suppose separations will be inevitable. But I believe that if the bonds are there, they will stay put in spite of stresses."

23

As Hilde Wangel in Ibsen's The Master Builder

Above. With Paul Scofield in Timon of Athens
Right. With husband Laurie Asprey
Far right. As Luciana in The Comedy of Errors

The stresses had begun when Packer won her Royal Shakespeare Company contract. She had signed on at the RSC elated but also ambivalent about accepting work as an actress that clearly outranked that of her husband. She had persuaded people at the RSC to audition Laurie Asprey as a member of the company and he had been accepted. But her schedule and her billing as compared with his made palpable their different statuses. Packer kept thinking that somehow she had failed to manage things properly, that it was all her fault.

Her husband was not her only colleague with a bruised ego: almost everyone she worked with had similar complaints. "It's very hard for people *not* to be unhappy in a theater group," she recalled. "I was happy but I saw other actors being promised roles and then not getting them. There would be a dispute about something, all the Associate Artists would meet to discuss it and find a solution, and then our director, Peter Hall, would say it was just not possible to use it. All of us would then get up in arms. I couldn't understand then why the greatest theater company in the world shouldn't also be the happiest.

"Now I'm more tolerant. I myself have, as a director of a company, taken actions that have had horrible consequences for other people. At the time, though, my idealism was constantly being shattered. My marriage was in a terrible state. I was drinking a bottle of wine a day. My husband was pressuring me not to stay with the Royal Shakespeare Company because he was so unhappy there and instead of ending my marriage, I got out of my contract with the RSC."

The leaving was officially explained by an offer Packer had received to play the lead in a BBC-TV adaptation of Charles Dickens' *David Copperfield*. Packer played Dora Spenlow against Ian McKellen's David in what was regarded as a prestigious serial. The television exposure gained her a wider

26

reputation and made for an interesting item on her resume, and it was while taping the fifth or sixth of the 14 episodes that she discovered that she was pregnant.

Tina Packer had not wanted to have a child during her twenties for all the reasons that a generation of women after her would postpone their childbearing. "It obviously would ruin my career!" she mimicked her younger self with glee years later. "It would destroy me as a sexual being! I would no longer be able to focus on my work!" Instead of growing thinner and frailer as her part called for, Packer got fatter and more robust. The director finally decided to rewrite Dickens and had Dora die in childbirth rather than of con-

sumption. The series and Tina Packer were both well-reviewed. "Tina Packer as Dora has got rid of some of that silly helplessness that I have come to expect from the role and she is making Dora the appealing girl Dickens must have meant her to be," wrote one critic. "I shall be sorry to see Dora go though usually I can't wait to see the back of her."

During her last months of pregnancy, Packer became what she later remembered fondly as "very bovine." Her husband became the family's chief breadwinner "which he liked" and the couple bought a home. In November of 1966, she gave birth to a son they named Jason and, for a few months, led the kind of domestic, routinized life that best nurtured her marriage. But motherhood, for Packer, seemed to infuse new energy into her professional and artistic life. "In practical terms," she later told younger women, "motherhood and a career are difficult to juggle. It sometimes looks and feels impossible when you have a dress rehearsal and your child—who has not had enough of your attention for that week anyway—absolutely wants and needs you at the same time. That does create a lot of tension. But I don't think I ever put my creativity to its full use until *after* I had Jason. It was as though I had to create biologically before I could be free to do artistic creation. Having a child got me to another level of consciousness of self. Everything I thought or felt somehow seemed more valid. I stopped worrying about what other people thought of me. I just didn't care anymore. I got a stronger identity of my own.

"I also think there's an odd side benefit. Because you are a woman raising a child, your career develops more slowly and that's not such a bad thing. You have the time to really think through what it is you want to do. You have the time to anticipate it. Jason's 18 now and soon I won't have him around at all. I anticipate a great release of energy will flow into my work."

28

Back in 1967, four and a half months after she gave birth, Packer went back to work in repertory theater. Her mother accompanied her wherever she was performing and took care of the baby; later, Packer would hire a series of nannies. But although she loved acting, Tina Packer grew restless with her work not long after resuming it. For the next four years, she played in repertory theaters, appeared on television, and even did a "trashy" film, slowly becoming as frustrated with her professional life as she was with her marital situation. After the high of performing Shakespeare with "the best company in the world," other playwrights and other companies dissatisfied her. She found herself fantasizing about "energy, color, space, a theater that moved" while moving from repertory theater to repertory theater,

and taking such roles as "brain drain scientist" for the BBC serial *Dr. Who* and "blonde nymphomaniac" for a contemporary play that scandalized its Scottish audiences. At one point, she appeared in the very tabloids she had so disdained as a Bohemian, on the inside pages, dressed in a mini-skirt, smiling for the camera.

Things came to a head while she was rehearsing a television adaptation of *The Heiress* by Henry James and the director realized he was running half an hour longer than his time slot allowed. Packer sensed that her part would be the one to be cut and seized upon the opportunity to end her acting career. "I walked out," she said. "I *left*. I demanded that they pay me since I was now playing a part that was not the one I had been offered. I was very stroppy. I had reached a point where I told myself: *either get out of the theater entirely or stop complaining and do what it is you want to do*. I got out. Then I left my husband too."

For about a year, "it was tough." She was 29 years old, mother of a small child, an actress with the most-coveted training in the English-speaking world, and no idea what to do with it. She settled in a cottage in Suffolk, a place she still uses as a retreat during "fallow periods." She supported herself, as she had during her times of unemployment as an actress, by writing for her old employer *Woman* Magazine. She sat around and walked and thought and tried to figure out what to do next.

"It took me time to focus and get courage. I knew what I *really* wanted to do was to develop my own style of doing Shakespeare. I realized I couldn't do that at the Royal Shakespeare—because there I was known as an actress and a junior person. I thought about going back to RADA, the drama school where I'd won the Ronson Award. They said: 'Absolutely Not!' However, there was another theater school where rather interesting people had taught and trained, including Kristin Linklater. That was LAMDA, the London Academy of Music and Dramatic Arts."

Among the half dozen leading drama schools in England at the time, LAMDA was known for being a bit looser and more open to innovation than the others. Founded primarily as a music conservatory, LAMDA was taken over in the mid-1950s by theater director Michael Macowan and a group of teachers who transformed it from a declining institution to a vital one. Smaller and more personal than the other drama schools, it was the first to add the methods of Stanislavski to traditional British training. While RADA still trained actors "from the outside in," according to Kristin Linklater, who was both a student and a teacher there, LAMDA had begun to investigate ways of working "from the inside out."

Packer went to LAMDA determined to talk herself into a position and in the spring of 1971, directed *Measure for Measure* there, followed by *The Winter's Tale*—an unusual choice for a fledgling director. The first was and has remained one of her favorite plays because it makes her laugh. "It juxtaposes the morality of the state and the way people struggle with their sexuality. I find the bawdy stuff *so funny,* and the struggle for a higher morality—the assumption that through your own will you can make morality work—so painful."

The Winter's Tale, regarded as "difficult" and "inaccessible" by many people, appealed to her because "it's so *powerful.* It's about faith and redemption. After 16 years of repentance, it's possible for a man to redeem his sin. The language is particularly beautiful. I like the balance of the poetic and the bawdy."

In the scrapbook that her mother still keeps, Packer pasted the programs of her first two productions. Then she wrote in clear letters: "End of Acting Career. Beginning of Directing Career."

Dick Kapp met Tina Packer about a year after she began directing at LAMDA. He was then working at the Ford Foundation as a program officer whose duties included writing rejection letters to the hundreds of people who submitted project ideas to the Division of Humanities and the Arts. Kapp did not regard himself as a Foundation bureaucrat. He had been a child prodigy, a pianist and conductor, a law student and an expatriate in Germany for many years before falling into his present job; he was a musician whose sympathies lay more with the people he was rejecting than with the organization he worked for.

One of the reasons Kapp was sending out so many form rejections was that the head of the theater division, MacNeil Lowry, had made a systematic study of the American theater scene a few years before to determine the country's "needs." As a result, the Foundation was funding about one dozen regional theaters including the Guthrie in Minneapolis, the Arena in Washington, D.C. and the Alley in Houston. But there was little money left over for projects that did not fit the funding structure that Lowry had put in place and Kapp found himself routinely rejecting very interesting ideas for purely administrative reasons.

32

Toward the end of 1971, Kapp received what he remembers as a "particularly cogent" letter from an Englishwoman directing at LAMDA which described a method of working on Shakespeare "through the emotion contained within the sound of the word itself." This idea so intrigued him that he wrote a personal reply and suggested to Tina Packer that they meet the next time he was in London. Within a few months they talked and Kapp returned to New York brimming with enthusiasm for Packer and her work. He talked about her to MacNeil Lowry who had already underwritten several women theater directors (theater people say that he believed women were better at nurturing companies along than men), and to other people in a position to help including George White, then president of the Eugene O'Neill Memorial Theater Center in Waterford, Connecticut. Kapp helped Packer write her first grant proposal and sailed it past all the barriers that had kept far better established theater people from getting Ford money. "We couched the proposal in the form of an experiment," he said later. "It was a very unusual grant. One hundred grand with which to pursue with

all artistic freedom communication of Shakespeare? There's no other one like it."

Packer had also written to Arthur Tortellot, a program officer at the CBS Foundation and a friend of one of her first great mentors, Harry Mathews, a novelist whom she had met as a teenager in France. Still wearing her ankle-length orange dress, she paid a visit to Tortellot at CBS and ultimately received an $11,000 grant. This experience with American foundations was totally new to her. In all of England, she thought, there were perhaps five foundations interested in funding the arts. In America, there were thousands. She threw herself into writing grant proposals with gusto and became so adept at the process that, unlike many artistic directors, she continued doing her own proposal writing for years.

Her style at the time was outrageously cheeky and ill-informed. There were, at the beginning of the 1970s, at least 20 other Shakespeare groups in North America with devoted followings. The oldest, the Oregon Shakespeare Festival in Ashland, had been started in 1935. The Old Globe Theater in San Diego, California, the Colorado Shakespeare Festival in Boulder, and the Folger Shakespeare Theater in Washington, D.C. were all respected institutions. Packer had never heard of them.

She did know that in North America, there were three very famous places that "did Shakespeare." One was the Stratford Festival in Ontario, Canada, which was then directed by fellow Briton Michael Langham and which, since 1953, had become Canada's chief cultural attraction. The second was the New York Shakespeare Festival which Joseph Papp had started in a church basement in 1954. Papp had become something of a folk hero in New York for bringing "free Shakespeare" to Central Park every summer since 1960, and his festival had evolved into the most exciting theater in the city. Packer had seen and liked Papp's musical version of *Two Gentlemen of Verona*. The third festival Tina Packer had heard of was the American Shakespeare Theater in Stratford, Connecticut, which had been drawing busloads of school children as well as adults from a tri-state area since 1955. But with a brashness that was as natural as it was staggering, she dismissed them all.

"I am aware that there are other companies doing Shakespeare," she wrote blithely in the grant proposal she finally submitted with Kapp's help in October of 1972, "but none are doing what we are doing. To take the most obvious examples, Mr. Papp's company and Mr. Langham's company: the former, while I admire the actors' vigor enormously and feel they often capture Shakespeare in spirit, are hard put to catch his soul because that is contained in the verse which Mr. Papp's men seem to fear; and the latter, while admirable in many respects, perpetuates the English Shakespearean acting tradition which even over here (in England) is obsolete and in the States can only be a false grafting without reference to the strong indigenous roots of American theater. And neither company has the intention, or the time, to explore new approaches to the text that require re-training in actual acting methods."

In pointing to the need for an American classical training, Packer had hit upon a sore spot. Despite the magnificent arts complexes that had been built all over North America, and despite the proliferation of drama schools at universities and conservatories, the training of actors in the United States did not produce the results obtained in Britain. Nearly every new tour by a British theater group was met with rave reviews from American critics and audiences as well as with articles that bemoaned the deficiencies of American theater.

Packer was playing her strongest suit when she wrote that, for the past year, she had been giving twelve American students at LAMDA classical Shakespearean training. "I have found that when Americans first come to me they are very mistrustful of words," she wrote. "However, once they are over this fear, they have a vigor and directness that English students do not seem to possess, and, in fact, are better able to express the depth and breadth of emotion felt by Shakespeare's characters. (I don't know whether this is because America is at this moment more closely in tune with Elizabethan England—in any case, that is a discussion we must leave for another time.) To the wealth of the word must be added the rhythm of the verse—when the emotion is right, the rhythm of the verse is right, and vice versa—which is a simple concept but takes some time to put into practice.

"The function of the clowns," she continued, "is of the utmost importance in Shakespeare's plays. The influence of the Commedia dell'Arte on Elizabethan theater, with its knockabout and improvised humor, cannot be overemphasized. There is not a play of Shakespeare's that does not have a strong comedy element (and some are a riot from beginning to end), but because of our inability to clown in the same manner, and because of the inordinate amount of 'seriousness' that has been attached to 'the Bard' much of the sheer joy and fun of Shakespeare has been lost for modern audiences. I have never met a school child who learned to love Shakespeare through lessons, a writer who is the most humane, funny and enlightened in English literature. The Americans I have been working with have already learned to relax in their attitude towards Him and are well into learning basic slapstick and tumbling techniques.

"The Shakespearean actor must be able to treat the audience as an integral part of the play," she continued. "To Shakespeare, the audience was the actor's alter ego. Thus, all the soliloquies are intended to be given directly to the audience. He allows the audience to 'know' as opposed to merely observe, the workings of a character's mind. Much of the comedy, too, is played directly to the audience. There must be an ease and naturalness about this that obviously can come about only by playing to audiences. The English students with whom I've been working have done much work in this field very successfully—and I can't wait to begin with the Americans."

Packer asked for six months in which to put this "experimental program of Shakespeare training" into practice: four months in England, where the young actors would rehearse; two months in America where they would perform. She asked for stipends for herself and members of her company, as well as salaries for the group of master teachers she had assembled by raiding the institutions where she had previously worked. She asked John Barton, her mentor from the Royal Shakespeare Company, to work on textual analysis and John Broome, who had been her movement teacher at RADA, to teach movement. She asked B. H. Barry, a colleague at LAMDA, to teach tumbling and combat and Kristin Linklater to teach voice. All agreed to be part of the project which John Broome remembers thinking was "a brilliant idea. There was no way to do it in England. England is a pretty poor country now. The arts budgets are cut back. And we have the RSC, which is regarded as having the ultimate in performing values: they weren't interested in a new approach. They'd say no, we've reached a state of perfection and in a way, they have. When Tina organized this, I was very keen to join."

Peter Hall, then director of the National Theater, endorsed the project in a letter to the Ford Foundation, noting Packer's "originality" and "drive" and adding that the "cross-fertilisation of new American talents with the craft and expertise of the English Shakespeare tradition is something that can do nothing but good."

In February of 1973, *Shakespeare & Company,* named after the English-language bookstore that Packer had frequented when she had lived in Paris, took up residence in the village of Alcester near Stratford-upon-Avon. There, actors and teachers embarked on a regimen of dawn to dusk training, designed to, in Packer's words, "find a way of doing Shakespeare that was both true to him and true to us." Although much was tried and discarded during those first six months, Packer's ideas about working with actors would remain essentially the same. Every morning, her company rose early and performed a series of exercises to "release the expressive power of the voice and body." Then the actors worked on texts, practiced clowning, tumbling, fighting, singing, dancing and, finally, their scenes.

Most of the elements of this training had existed long before Packer was born. Kristin Linklater would later trace its roots to acting traditions in France, Germany, Russia and England. What characterized *Shakespeare & Company* from its inception was its highly eclectic curriculum, the dovetailing of its parts, and the cohesion of its teachers who have all remained associated with it since 1973. "Some other British drama schools are a bit staid, controlled, overorganized," said John Broome, trying to pinpoint the difference for himself. "You move from one class to another without feeling a link. Most theater schools will have a fight director, voice people, and movement people. But each subject is in its own compartment. In this company, it's one organic whole.

"The other big difference here is in the approach to the the text. They treat Shakespeare like an actor who wrote in lots of cues for other actors: for them, he's an actor's writer rather than an intellectual's writer. At the RSC, most of the directors are university men. They are excellent and they often state that they do not take the erudite approach but they cannot escape the fact that they are intellectuals. For

38

me, Tina's approach is freer. It revitalizes the language and revitalizes the bodies that are speaking the language rather than concentrating on the concept."

Broome and his colleague Trish Arnold, who taught at LAMDA and would later join the company, were both former dancers. Their ideas about movement derived from the Ballet Joos, founded in Germany during the Weimar Republic. Kurt Joos had been interested in exploring the "harmony of the body" instead of set dance forms. His techniques were brought to England by Sigurd Leder who taught them to Broome and Arnold. The philosophy behind them was a perfect complement to the voice work that Kristin Linklater had developed.

Linklater had trained at LAMDA with Michael Macowan as her mentor. She became the protegée and heir apparent to Iris Warren, one of the teachers who had come to LAMDA in the 1950s with Macowan. Like Packer, Linklater had been told by her teachers that she was not quite right for leading roles in Shakespeare. They said she would come "into her own" in her thirties. As a result, Linklater became a voice teacher even before she had graduated from school and, by 1973, had made it her life.

She traced the roots of her ideas about voice to the ancient Greeks. "In Greece," she told her students, "the job of the actor was to go onstage and, by creating harmonious sounds, reinforce the harmonies of the spheres. This is a role that involves far more than telling stories or enlightening people or serving as a vehicle for their catharsis. It can be achieved only by the alignment of the body and the soul. The Greeks believed they could do this. The Elizabethans took a passionate interest in the Greeks and their search for harmony imbues their theater. But over the centuries, that original search for the oneness between man and the universe that took place in the Globe Theater has evolved into set speeches,

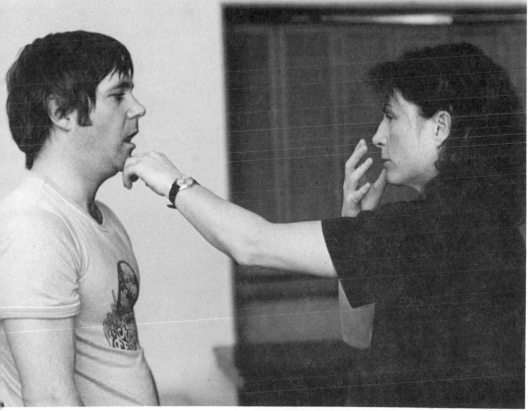

empty forms of elocution and an emphasis on correct diction."

Like the movement teachers who wished to unearth the impulses that had resulted in ballet, Linklater and her teacher Iris Warren, excavated the sources of declamatory speech.

Iris Warren was teaching at RADA in the early 1930s when, according to Linklater, she fell in love with an Austrian psychoanalyst who had studied with Freud. He asked Warren to help some of his patients talk about themselves more freely and Warren discovered that, as they let their inhibitions drop and their emotions emerge, their voices changed. She began to apply what she had learned from the psychoanalytic patients to her acting students.

"Now you have to understand," Kristin Linklater said, "that in those days in England, no one ever had a 'nervous breakdown' or 'went to a shrink.' People 'went away for a while.' And in drama schools, people did not work from the inside out. In those days, the idea was to do everything beautifully. You entered, kept your eyes on the audience, closed the door behind you, walked forward talking and at the same time feeling with your calf for the chair so that you could sit down beautifully without taking your eyes off the audience and continue talking—never missing a beat. You had to practice that a great deal. Not knocking over the furniture was a major goal, as was making pear-shaped vowels."

Iris Warren had abandoned all that by the time she taught Kristin Linklater at LAMDA. Instead, she worked intensively on breathing from the diaphragm, on straightening the spine and on "unlocking" the natural voice. The results were excellent. Actors were able to project better in large halls, to control their voices better, and allow themselves all kinds of nuance. Linklater built on Warren's work and became enormously successful in the U.S. as a "speech consultant" who was called in to help actors be heard in the huge arts complexes that were built throughout the country during the 1960s and 1970s. But the work she did was usually on one play or with one cast of actors. Tina Packer was the first director Linklater had encountered who did not merely ask her in for a few weeks, but who embraced the techniques and literally incorporated them into her training of actors. Both women disliked the "phony" theatrical voices that some drama schools encouraged by setting a "correct" standard of speech. The two women insisted that the actor free his natural voice and discover its strengths rather than try to imitate an external standard.

"I had worked with a lot of directors who respected what I did, but what I heard in the final result was never even close to the potential for expression which I knew was possible," said Linklater. "That's because most directors *tell* their actors what to do and the actors try to do it. My job would be helping the director fulfill his vision when often I might not even agree with this vision. I would never be following through on what the actor or I might find in the text. With Tina, I felt that this was exactly what she *needed* from me."

At Alcester during the first months of *Shakespeare & Company,* Packer and Linklater worked with actors in pairs or as a group, experimenting with a technique they called "dropping in the word." They fed the actors one word at a time, had them imagine that they were breathing the word into their bodies, and asked them to let the word play on emotions and memory. This way of probing the text had several results. It facilitated memorization of lines, it initiated an immediate emotional relationship between actors working on the same scene and it allowed them to viscerally experience the meaning of the words Shakespeare had written. It produced a kind of musicality and reciprocity between

44

players that is more characteristic of chamber musicians than actors. And it reinforced Packer's emphasis on the primacy of the concrete rather than abstract nature of Shakespeare's language.

Once the words had "played on and through the actors," John Barton, the former Cambridge don who had been Packer's mentor at the Royal Shakespeare Company, did a more conventional analysis of the structure of the verse, teaching the actors to read the clues in the written text by speaking the verse and examining the implications of punctuation, line endings and meter.

To the work on voice and body was added the fight and tumbling training of B. H. Barry who taught the actors an Elizabethan stage vocabulary. "The whole point of being an actor," said Tina Packer, "is to be able to do many more things than an ordinary mortal can do." Barry taught his students to climb the sides of walls and feel safe when it looked as though they were choking or pummeling each other.

A reporter from a Birmingham paper who visited Alcester in February of 1973 came away impressed with the number of highly-respected theater teachers involved with such an experimental company as well as with the packed schedule of classes. By April, the group was performing. Because their work permit did not allow them to put on commercial productions, they gave free previews of *The Taming of the Shrew*. *The Stratford-upon-Avon Herald* reviewed them as "Fast, furious, riotous and ribald . . ." and noted that they drew "on modes associated with Italy, which naturally enough have been developed in America as well as in Europe. There are hints of Wild Western knock-about and more than a touch of the Grouchos."

Elated, the actors left England in June and took up residence at the O'Neill Center in Waterford, Connecticut where

45

Packer, her son, parents and two actor friends in 1973

problems began. There were housing problems (the actors objected to living at O'Neill facilities and voted to rent two houses which turned out to be too small for their needs). There were financial problems (a mix-up over salaries and *per diems* had left the actors and their families with almost no pocket money). There were union problems (some of the actors, now that they were back in the U.S., wanted to join Equity; others wished to retain their student status). There were also the nagging personal problems—unhappiness, hysteria, insecurity, jealousy—that occur in every group but seem to plague theater companies in particular.

Tina Packer had founded her company with an underlying political philosophy then characteristic of many theater people in England. She viewed things, according to Linklater, "from a typical British left-wing humanist Marxist viewpoint," which is to say that she loathed the display of authority. As a young actress at the RSC and as a student, she had worked in companies run by men and she had sworn that were she to run a company, it would be run differently. The trouble was she had no model. There were only two women directors whose work she knew and admired. One was Ariane Mnouchkine in Paris; the other was Joan Littlewood in London. Packer did not know how Mnouchkine ran her company but she did know that Joan Littlewood had failed to transform her "bawdy, wonderful working-class theater" into a durable institution. In Alcester, she told her actors that *Shakespeare & Company* would be run as a democracy, with one vote assigned to every member. "I thought that as an actor, you were responsible for your performance and that you ought to be responsible in other parts of your life as well," Packer recalled ruefully. At the time, she had no experience with psychotherapy or group dynamics or management techniques.

She was also unaware of the toll that directing a new

46

company and moving it from England to America would take on herself. She was then 35 years old, separated from her husband, and responsible for a small child. She had a lover, Austin Hyslop, who had recently been told by his doctors that he had cancer. Hyslop was "an actor from Glasgow, a working-class boy, strictly Catholic, a great stand-up comic," who lived in London. He and Packer had agreed that she should go on to America and return to England only in the event that Hyslop's doctors told him that he was close to death.

Tina Packer tried to handle all of this with typical good cheer. She left her son in the care of her mother, said good-bye to Hyslop, and tended to her company's problems as though they were her own. Applying her political philosophy, she scheduled company meetings so that everything could be discussed in a "democratic" way, meetings that became so long (one lasted 24 hours) and so frequent that they began to destroy morale, displace rehearsals, and shift the center of attention from Shakespeare to company politics. According to outside evaluators who were called in to assess the project, a few actors began to dominate the group and Packer, struggling to find a style of leadership that suited her, was unable to hold the group together. Everything she had ever been taught, as well as her staunch identification with the working class, had prejudiced her against "establishment rules" and "authoritarianism," by which she meant "taking charge." Later, she described herself as "utterly incapacitated" and "truly shocked" as she watched four months of training dribble away during interminable group gripe sessions which she herself had set up.

"I felt so disillusioned with human behavior that I couldn't function properly," she remembered years later. "Here were the people I was working so closely with to do the thing dearest to me—destroying one another. I find it very difficult to terminate things but finally I wound up firing one of the people. That was the first positive thing I did. Just before we were set to begin performances. A second person left the company in support of the first."

The original plan of performing *King Lear* and *The Winter's Tale* was scrapped and the company, minus two key players, performed only *The Taming of the Shrew*. They played at the O'Neill Center in Waterford, then in New London, Connecticut, then in East Hampton, Long Island, before taking the play to the Performing Garage in New York City. In the eyes of some of the Ford Foundation's outside evaluators, all the excitement about a new approach failed to materialize onstage. The major New York papers did not send reviewers. The critics who did come were not bowled over and at least one was savage. "The more you love Shakespeare, the more you'll loathe what this company is doing to him," wrote the reviewer for the *Mamaroneck Times* under a headline that read SHAKESPEARE COMPANY SLAPS(STICK) THE BARD. "At this stage of their development, the performers are better acrobats than actors. Much of the clowning is pathetically unfunny, and only at infrequent moments is the acting effective." *WNBC News* called it "violent, sexy, full of action . . . an experiment that works." The *Village Voice* was the only paper of significance to review the show and, while its critic acknowledged that the group was "very skilled at physical and musical fooling" he asked, "How much is enough?"

As Dick Kapp said later, "Tina had assumed she would be greeted as the Second Coming and instead she got a couple of reviews and went down without a ripple." MacNeil Lowry, at the Ford Foundation, told her there would be no more money forthcoming: the experiment was over. That week Packer received a telegram from Austin Hyslop, asking her to come back to London.

48

She flew back immediately and, ten days later, Hyslop died. Packer collected her son and retreated to her cottage in the country. Every plan she had made in the last year was now irrelevant; her confidence was gone. For a while she did nothing. Nothing at all.

Most of the year that followed the demise of the first *Shakespeare & Company* falls into the category of what Packer calls a "fallow" period. She has had several of these periods during her career, considers them "necessary" and freely tells other artists about the days that she stayed in bed until noon, read or stared out the windows wondering: is this what I was born to do?

"At that point, in the winter of 1973–74, I thought I'd really had it," she recalled. "I didn't understand anything anymore. I didn't go down to London, didn't work, didn't call anyone. That total seclusion lasted for about three months. For some reason, I had put away some money so that at least I could live, if I lived frugally. So I got new curtains. I put in some linoleum. I had the rhythm of getting Jason off to school in the mornings and being there in the afternoons when he came home, so that was good. But I did not know what to do. I had had my opportunity to experiment with the kinds of things I thought would work in theater and they did. But the things that I thought about life didn't work at all.

"I thought that if you gave an individual the tools of his trade, good living conditions, and the opportunity to speak his mind, happiness would automatically ensue. Those ten months had shown me that was not true, that unconscious drives were far more powerful in everyone—including myself—than any idealistic vision of human behavior. It hadn't registered with me until then that people have committed every sin in the world under the guise of political idealism. I knew that was true of religion, that the Crusades, for example, were brutal and not at all 'Christian' but it took me longer to see that the same thing was true in politics.

"Still, I didn't have it in my bones to run a company the way I had seen them run—by a boss. I didn't know if I should give up theater entirely. How else could I earn a living? Should I go back to journalism? I didn't want to. A friend of mine came over from New York and talked about setting up another Shakespeare company and I went through the motions with him but it couldn't really take root. I talked to Dick Kapp over the phone. I wrote to Mac Lowry. Everyone said: put your ideas down on paper but I found it very difficult to put *anything* down on paper. Then Dick suggested a Travel/Study grant. The Ford Foundation would pay me to look around and see what it was I needed."

Packer's son, Jason, was seven years old by then. His best friend as well as his cousin had gone off to boarding school and he now began pestering his mother to be sent away to school too. "Boarding school is far more common in England than it is in America," Packer explained later about sending the boy off at such an early age. "There was nothing extraordinary about doing it and I really didn't have any ambivalence in the beginning since he wanted to go. It was only a question of finding one that Jason liked. The first year I felt fine because he was so happy. Then he decided he didn't like it and that was hard."

Packer arranged her travels to be with Jason during school vacations. She said she started to understand then that if she acknowledged that she had no idea what she wanted, then maybe she could view her travels as a way of finding some answer. Again, however, she had to put together a grant proposal. And, unlike many other people who have found themselves in a similar situation and have been unable to make themselves write one, Packer did. "I had to put together a proposal based on theater, although the questions I had were to do with life," she said matter-of-factly. "So I talked with Dick and we concocted this thing: I wanted to go to India to find out about the relationship between Sanskrit verse and music and to see the Tomasha, Jatra, Kathkali and Sanskrit theaters. I wanted to go to Israel to meet with Moshe Feldenkreis and learn about his work with movement: how realignment of the body realigns the mind. I wanted to see how Peter Brook was working in Paris and what they did at Milan's Theatro Piccolo and at the Berliner Ensemble in Berlin. I wanted to go across America because I was nearly illiterate about American theater.

"I had to go to New York to see Dick Kapp and Lowry and I thought: while I'm over there, I'll do one of those things Americans do to see if I can't get out of this depression. I had got in mind something like primal screaming."

She chuckled. "I had never done any therapy before but I wanted something fast and violent. I thought that unless it was really intense it wouldn't shift me; I had gotten too clever at finding reasons why things couldn't be changed. I got to Kristin's apartment just as she had to leave for Scotland because her father was dying. Just as she was leaving, she said there was someone coming round to tell her about something called *est* training. She said: you do it in two weekends, it's very violent, and it changes your life. I said: good, lots of screaming, they lock you in a room so that you can't go to the loo—just the opposite of the way I'd been running my company. The next night I went to a seminar and that weekend, I was in training."

52

The *est* training, along with primal scream therapy, gestalt therapy and some two hundred other ways of tapping into the "human potential movement" had hit New York with great force. It affected businesspeople, educators, athletes—people in almost every line of work. But actors, particularly, found its methods directly applicable to their craft. Tina Packer seized upon *est* with the unabashed fervor of a religious convert. "I understood for the first time that you are not what you *think*. I had never before really understood that there was a difference between the voice in your head and your actual state of being," she said. "Maybe that's obvious to most people but it wasn't to me." Packer refers to the various American therapies as "enlightenment," and some of the evangelical flavor of *est* and its brusque way of developing intimate group dynamics can be felt in Packer's training methods today.

Packer both retained her sense of humor about "enlightenment forms" and took from them whatever she found useful. Her own family had not touched a great deal and, despite their progressiveness, had neither screamed nor confessed in public the way Americans were now routinely doing. Her long impatience with British "repression" now came to a head and her sense that "sex and violence on stage was a cathartic experience for both actor and audience" was bolstered by what was becoming, in some American circles, admirable behavior. She, Kristin Linklater, and many of the others who later joined her were Rolfed, Alexandered, rebirthed, and exposed to several varieties of talking therapy. By the time the second *Shakespeare & Company* emerged in 1978, the handling of administrative and artistic problems would be aided by a psychological sophistication entirely absent from the first.

After spending a few months in America in 1974, Tina Packer went to India. Like many young Westerners of the time, she had read some Krishnamurti and Alan Watts, had heard stories of the guru Muktananda, and believed that India would be her spiritual home. Instead, still not recovered from the events of the previous year, Packer found herself falling apart in a succession of Indian hotel rooms. The streets of Bombay and Calcutta terrified her. She was unprepared for the masses of people, the poverty, the filth, the illness. At Muktananda's ashram, she was intrigued by watching the guru "energize" his disciples but when he touched her forehead, all that happened was that she contracted "a splitting headache that lasted for two days." Alienated from her own culture and uncomprehending of the one she was in, Packer veered between horror at people who "spit on each other's feet" and horror at her own shaky sense of self. She spent hours in her hotel rooms rereading Krishnamurti and trying to stay calm through what she vaguely understood was a severe personal crisis. What she says she retained from the Indian experience is a sense of her own strength and the necessity of ceding control and "allowing things to happen," instead of resisting them. She often tells actors about the day she went into the countryside with a troupe of Bengali actors who, after their perfomance, asked her to do some Shakespeare for them.

They knew no English. After struggling with the futility of trying to do anything for a few minutes, she launched into the speech the Princess of France makes in the last act of *Love's Labours Lost*. In it, the Princess responds to an offer of marriage from the King of Navarre who has attempted a life of monastic seclusion and failed. She tells him that she will consider his proposal in a year's time, after he has had the opportunity to prove his resolve a second time:

> Go with speed
> To some forlorn and naked hermitage
> Remote from all the pleasures of the world

There stay until the twelve celestial signs
Have brought about the annual reckoning
If this austere insociable life
Change not your offer made in heat of blood
If frosts and fasts, hard lodging and thin weeds
Nip not the gaudy blossoms of your love
But that it bear this trial and last love
Then at the expiration of the year,
Come challenge me, challenge me by these deserts
And by this virgin palm now kissing thine
I will be thine. . . .

"I knew that speech really well," Packer tells actors, "and I loved it because it's about having the strength to endure and to wait. There's something about really sticking with things that I have always found important. At the end of the play, he goes off to a monastery and she goes off to France, to rule the country. I suppose there's something about that situation that appeals to me as well!"

The Bengalis applauded her. She herself felt that something of the feeling of the speech had gotten across. Her experiences in India, she said, taught her about "the will to communicate" and the importance of "allowing things to happen." Both ideas influenced her style as a director and the phrase "Allow yourself to . . ." became a frequent refrain in her coaching of actors.

At intervals during her Foundation-funded travels, she flew back to England to spend school vacations with her son. The original plan of one year's travel and study became two years. She returned to New York and London between trips, cementing her personal and professional ties to Kristin Linklater, John Broome, B. H. Barry and Trish Arnold. These people not only helped her regain her confidence but arranged for her to do occasional workshops at the institutions where they had ties. Slowly, Packer garnered enough energy and faith in herself to try again to create another company.

"I started coming back to life again in a very sheltered environment, through the universities," she recalled. Through Linklater, she was hired at New York University to do a project on violence, "The Wars of the Roses," which drew on parts of *Henry VI, Richard the II* and *Richard the III*. "I did *Romeo and Juliet* at SUNY. I did *Lear* in London. I wasn't doing anything of the weight I had done before but, bit by bit, I started getting excited again. I could feel I had gotten to another level just in my exchange with people. You don't always learn things at the time you think you learn them. Some things become clear six months or a year after they have happened to you. You start teaching and the people you teach begin to teach you back. Slowly, I understood that it would be impossible to do the kind of theater I wanted to do at another institution. I had approached the Royal Shakespeare Company about directing there and the National Theater had thought there were funds for me to work there, but in the end the money fell through. I realized that I had to start my own company."

The rudiments were already in place. Packer called on the group of master teachers with whom she had worked in 1973 and who had remained enthusiastic about her way of doing theater. In addition, she had since worked with a number of actors at various universities who were anxious to continue under her direction. One of them was Dennis Krausnick, who was finishing his M.F.A at New York University in January of 1976. He decided to participate in Packer's "Wars of the Roses" project for his final semester.

Krausnick had been raised in Scottsbluff, Nebraska and had entered a Jesuit novitiate straight out of high school. Throughout his years of religious study, he retained a strong interest in the theater and, after he had been ordained a priest, the Wisconsin Province of the Society of Jesus agreed

to send him to drama school. His two years in New York had been full ones: he studied voice with Kristin Linklater, worked on his acting, and continued to function as a priest, hearing confessions at a Long Island church on weekends. His first contact with Tina Packer was electric. "She was talking about love and hate as I came in—late—to her class," he recalled. "And about how the function of theater was to heal. I fell in love with her."

Packer tends to have a profound effect on people around her but this time, she set in motion the then 34-year-old Krausnick's struggle to decide whether or not to remain a priest. Packer returned to England that summer. Krausnick took a year off from work to stay in New York, do some therapy and sort out his status within the church. By 1978, he had decided to leave the Jesuits. Soon after, he and Packer moved in together and, with Kristin Linklater, began planning how to set up the new company. The not-for-profit theater movement was booming in the United States, encouraged in part by the success of the New York Shakespeare Festival which had managed to put three of its productions, *Hair, A Chorus Line* and *For Colored Girls . . .* on Broadway. There was no dearth of models to follow now and, as Kristin Linklater recalled, "we thought we would be sensible and do it the right way."

The right way in the minds of all concerned was to follow the example set by Tyrone Guthrie, the charismatic English director. He had canvassed the United States, looking for a community that could afford and would support a full-scale repertory theater, and had settled on Minneapolis, Minnesota. First he put in place a triumverate: an artistic director, an administrative director and a managing director. Second, he got together a board of directors who went out and raised plenty of money. Third, he built a theater. Fourth, he chose the plays. Fifth, he hired the actors. This, the master teachers

Dennis Krausnick directing in 1984

of *Shakespeare & Company* agreed, was how they, too, should proceed.

Kristin Linklater, who was then 41, had just had a baby. Since a theater was at least one year away, she decided to go home to Scotland, introduce her child to her family and "be just a mother for a while." Packer, then 39, with an eleven-year-old son in boarding school, would continue to do workshops in America and England, and would follow the Guthrie model, primarily by looking for money.

In April of 1978, according to plan, Packer was directing a production of Molière's *The Learned Ladies* at Smith College in Northampton, Massachusetts. She kept in close touch with Dick Kapp. It was on a weekend visit to Chappaqua, New York, where Kapp then lived, that *Shakespeare & Company* found the man who would find it a home. As Kapp remembered it, he had asked his neighbor, a former longshoreman and a successful real estate developer, to come over and meet Tina Packer. Mitch Berenson had retained the style of a longshoreman long after he had moved on to a more lucrative livelihood. When Packer walked into Kapp's home, she assumed he was helping a third man fix the skylight in Kapp's roof. All four of them stood in the kitchen for a while chatting over coffee and Packer began talking about India and her various theater projects of the past few years.

Mitch Berenson wanted to know why she didn't have a permanent place to work. Packer told him that she had asked for a place within the Royal Shakespeare Company as well as in the National Theater. The National had at first expressed interest but some expected funding had not come through and there was simply no money. "Most directors spend $100,000 on costumes and I spend $8," she told him. "But I need money for master teachers and that's very expensive. I also need a place to perform."

About three days later, Berenson telephoned Packer to offer his assistance. He drove up to Smith College, sat in on rehearsals of *The Learned Ladies,* and like the many observers who would later be impressed with Packer's methods, felt inspired by what he saw. Berenson was at a point in his life when he had money and energy to spare: here was a project he could pour himself into with gusto. Beyond Berenson's enthusiasm for Packer's work was a basic understanding between the two. Both saw themselves as anti-

61

establishment outsiders—he, the former longshoreman; she, the former beatnik expatriate. Neither had attended college. Both had succeeded in their lives without the benefit of academic credentials and old-boy networks. Moreover, like Packer, Berenson trusted his instincts and acted on them immediately. He told her that her theater should be in Berkshire County, about an hour's drive west of Smith College.

Packer had never heard of the Berkshires. Berenson told her they were a set of high rolling hills dotted with lakes and ponds where many New Yorkers and Bostonians kept second homes. There was a local population of about 75,000 year-round residents, several private schools, and, most importantly, a tradition of supporting the arts. The Boston Symphony Orchestra, he told her, spent its summers on an old

estate called Tanglewood, named after a collection of stories that the American novelist Nathaniel Hawthorne had written while a resident in Lenox, Massachusetts. Young musicians from all over the world now came to Tanglewood for advanced training in composition, conducting, singing and performing. There was a summer dance festival in nearby Becket that had been founded in 1933. There was one well-known summer theater in Williamstown and another in Stockbridge. The popular American painter Norman Rockwell had lived and painted in that town, as had the sculptor Daniel Chester French, whose sculpture of Abraham Lincoln sat in the Lincoln Memorial in Washington, D.C. Herman Melville had written *Moby Dick* in Pittsfield, Edith Wharton had written half a dozen novels in Lenox, and the poet Edna St. Vincent Millay had lived just across the state line in Hillsdale, New York. Artists seemed to gravitate toward the Berkshires. It also seemed to be a region where women had been able to find the conditions they needed to do what they wished to do.

Tanglewood had, in fact, been created by a woman: Gertrude Robinson Smith of New York City. Miss Robinson Smith was the daughter of a Wall Street lawyer. Raised on Sutton Place, she became one of those wealthy, independent, socially impeccable women one encounters in the novels of Henry James. During World War I, she raised money for medical equipment and ice-making machinery to send to the Allied Forces and was subsequently named to the French Legion of Honor for her efforts. With her life-long companion, Miriam Oliver, she built her own summer house near Stockbridge and maintained an active interest in various women's organizations. She was 53 when conductor Henry Hadley came to her for help in organizing a summer music festival in the Berkshires.

It was 1934, the middle of the Great Depression, but within

a few weeks Gertrude Robinson Smith had galvanized the rich and famous of Berkshire County to transform a horse ring on a neighboring farm into an arena for concerts. Sixty-five members of the New York Philharmonic-Symphony Orchestra were bussed up from Manhattan to Stockbridge that summer and lodged for free in the area's hotels. Some of Robinson Smith's society friends put up money to offset the deficit they were sure would result at the end of the project. The Junior League of Pittsfield sold refreshments. Various prominent people including President Franklin D. Roosevelt's mother attended the first of three summer concerts. Gertrude Robinson Smith took care to ensure that her festival would be read about all over the country. In addition to cultivating the attention of the *Berkshire Eagle,* Pittsfield's newspaper, she advertised in the *New York Times* and the *New York Herald Tribune.* The concerts of 1934 were thus judged a success by an audience well beyond the Berkshires.

For a series of reasons documented in Herbert Kupferberg's *Tanglewood,* things did not work out with the New York orchestra and their conductor. Miss Robinson Smith set out to woo Serge Koussevitzky, the Russian-born conductor of the Boston Symphony Orchestra since 1924. She persuaded him to give up his summers in France to conduct in the Berkshires. By 1938, Koussevitzky was conducting in a music shed designed by the architect Eliel Saarinen. The audience would soon number in the tens of thousands. Tanglewood would become one of the most famous music festivals in the world, the proving ground of such artists as Leonard Bernstein, Sarah Caldwell and Seiji Ozawa, and a pillar of social and economic life in Berkshire County.

Packer had never heard of Gertrude Robinson Smith when she set out theater-hunting in the Berkshires with Mitch Berenson in the spring of 1978. It was odd to be spending

64

hours alone in a car with a man she had just met, driving through unfamiliar countryside. But Dick Kapp had encouraged her to accept Mitch Berenson's offer to find her a theater. So she sat back and looked out at the thawing Berkshire landscape which was just on the verge of turning green.

The idea of starting a company in an outlying county did not strike Packer as outlandish. Stratford-upon-Avon was, after all, two hours by train from London—just a bit closer than the Berkshires were to New York City. Although many people assume that the Royal Shakespeare Company dates back to Shakespeare's time, Packer knew that the Memorial Theater in Stratford had been constructed just over one hundred years ago. For several decades, Londoners had looked down on its productions with that special disdain city people everywhere reserve for summer festival theater. A fire destroyed the Memorial in 1925 and George Bernard Shaw was said to have telegraphed his congratulations. With financial help from the United States, a new theater was opened in 1932 but it was not until the 1950s that Stratford began to acquire the august reputation that it enjoys today. During that decade, directors Peter Brook, Anthony Quayle, and Glen Byam Shaw came to Stratford, bringing with them actors Laurence Olivier, Paul Scofield, John Gielgud, Michael Redgrave and Peggy Ashcroft. Each year, a different group was assembled until 1960, when director Peter Hall took over. It was during the time of Hall's innovations that Tina Packer had been hired to work at Stratford, becoming part of what was then an infant company. Hall renamed the funereal-sounding Memorial Theater and its productions the Royal Shakespeare Company, and secured a London stage in the Aldwych Theater.

Packer thought of Stratford as Mitch Berenson drove her through the Berkshires, looking at theaters. They saw one empty one near Tanglewood which she disliked. Then the two went to have a drink at the Red Lion Inn in Stockbridge where someone suggested they look at the 100-seat theater that stood on the grounds of Foxhollow, a local resort. They looked at the building but Packer felt it was far too small. It was on a dirt road going back to Route 7 that Packer suddenly was drawn to a large mansion that she glimpsed through the car window. It was barely visible in the twilight and was surrounded by snow. They inquired and were told that the place was called The Mount, and that it was about seventy years since an American woman, the novelist Edith Wharton, had built it. She had lived there for twelve years. Then a succession of owners held it. "There were no keys and it was boarded up—no one had lived there for a long time," Packer recalled. "The next day, we went and looked at it properly. I *really* liked it. All the shutters were shut. There was ice all over the floor from a hundred different

Shakespeare & Company Presents
Edith Wharton:
An Intimate Portrait
by Karen Shreefter

For The Benefit Of
Edith Wharton Restoration, Inc.

Far right. The Mount

Edith Wharton adaptation playbill

leaks in broken pipes. The library was knee-deep in books and there wasn't a room without plaster out. You could see the bare slats in the walls. It was filthy and freezing cold. None of it made any difference to me. I knew I wanted *this* house. It had a real identity. Nothing else I had seen had that."

At the time Packer was ignorant of Edith Wharton's work although, by coincidence, she had lived on Rue de Varennes, across the street from Wharton's Paris residence, during the time she had spent in France. Later on Packer read that Edith Wharton had been ill for twelve years before moving to The Mount and that once she settled in, did some of her best writing. She believes that she felt Wharton's energy in the walls of The Mount and a sense of her spirit hovering over the grounds.

Part of what Tina Packer felt was the result of an architecture and interior design that Wharton had thought through

after writing her first (non-fiction) book, *The Decoration of Houses,* in 1897. The model for it was an English country estate. "The house has a powerful feminine quality but not like a nunnery," said Packer who has since read almost everything Edith Wharton ever published and much about her as well. "She built it in order to communicate with other people. Each of the rooms—except her bedroom—has several entrances so that people can get in and out without seeing anyone they don't wish to see. And each room is intimate. You can be cozy if you want; you can be solitary if you want. She was really interested in how spaces affect people and their interaction with each other, and she imprinted the house with her kind of harmony. There are no distractions there. The architecture itself sets a standard of excellence. It stretches you. You don't want to do shoddy work there because the people who worked there before you reached out all the time."

Wharton built The Mount in 1901 as a refuge from what she saw as "the flat frivolity" of Newport, Rhode Island, where her husband Teddy and most of their social set spent their summers. Wharton's marriage was, by that time, strained by her literary ambitions as well as by a basic incompatibility between husband and wife. She spent much of her time at The Mount attended only by servants. Writing long-hand in bed every morning (her secretary would gather completed pages from the floor), Wharton completed several novels. In the library, she often conversed with guests Henry James or Bernard Berenson. On the grounds she had entertained the *London Times* correspondent Morton Fullerton who became her lover when she was 45. Edith Wharton had travelled to Nohant, in France, to see the environment that another woman writer, George Sand, had ordered so that she could best do her work. Now Tina Packer walked through the house that Edith Wharton had designed for the same reason.

Rationally, Tina Packer said later, it was stupid to even consider The Mount as a home for *Shakespeare & Company*. It was very cold. Even in the middle of April the water on the floors inside the house was frozen solid. Edith Wharton herself always left the Berkshires in December and stayed away until June. The mansion would be enormously expensive to heat. But Packer thought about another stately home she had recently seen, the building that housed the Glyndebourne Festival in England. She liked it. True, Edith Wharton had neglected to build a theater on the grounds but she, Tina Packer, could add one. The new theater company would need office space, workshop space, dressing rooms and living quarters for the actors—not one of whom came from the Berkshires. Living and working at The Mount could prove to be a cohesive force for the company. Impulse took over and Tina Packer told Mitch Berenson she had found her theater.

According to the sensible Guthrie model, the search for a theater was to have taken about a year. Instead, Packer and Berenson discovered that The Mount was on the market. They could rent it for the summer, retaining an option to buy later on. "Another party was interested," said Packer. "I felt the ship was sailing: we had better get on. So we rented it. Mitch told his friend Herb Halpern about it and they got a good deal on the rent because Mitch agreed to do the necessary repairs. We got it for $8,000 plus $4,000 worth of labor."

The Ford Foundation was then in the midst of changing officers but, once again, came through for Packer—this time with a $5,000 personal grant which would allow her to set things up in Lenox. The money that Berenson and Halpern contributed for the rent was funneled through a non-profit cultural foundation that Dick Kapp had previously set up for his own artistic venture: The New York Philharmonia

Virtuosi. It was the first time Tina Packer learned that "in order for people to give you money, you need non-profit status and for that you need a lawyer." The group found one who became a member of its board.

One week after first glimpsing The Mount, she returned with Dennis Krausnick who remembers being left alone in the courtyard with a key, a tape measure and a flashlight. His instructions were to make a floorplan of the mansion and determine where 25 company members could live. "There were clumps of *arborvitae* 12 feet high covering the windows," he recalled, "and the shutters—about 60 pairs of shutters—had been closed for two years. There was molding food in various parts of the house amid the dirt and plaster, and in the refrigerator was a dead pizza. I would enter a room, try to pry open a shutter for light. Then I'd get down on my hands and knees with my tape measure, write down the measurements, then jump up and down to get warm."

Krausnick had almost completed his map of the third floor when he heard the sound of steps coming from the floor below. They echoed in the empty house and made Krausnick so uneasy that he began tiptoeing around, listening. His first thought was that some derelict was camping out on the second floor. Then he realized he was thinking like a New Yorker, that it was either some Edith Wharton fanatic who had followed him into the house or some tourist with car trouble looking for a telephone. In New York, he had developed the habit of stopping before entering his apartment in the East Village and calling out: "Hello! If you don't belong here, get out please!" as a warning to housebreakers. He did that now and the footsteps stopped. There was not a sound.

"I went down to the second floor," Krausnick recalled, "and I checked out each room with my flashlight, throwing open the closet doors, getting hit with a cloud of plaster and

70

whatever else happened to be in the closet, scaring the daylights out of myself. It finally dawned on me that what I was doing was useless. Edith Wharton had designed her house in such a way that anyone could leave any room by a second exit. I got very rattled. I had never believed in ghosts. I finished up the floorplan in a rush and waited for Tina down in the courtyard. The next time I went up there from New York, my car broke down before I got out of the city and then I drove up the whole way on Route 7 because I didn't want to get lost and I knew it was just off Route 7. When I finally got there, it was four in the morning, there was a bright moon, and the house was gleaming like a painting. I parked in the courtyard, turned off my lights and realized I couldn't possibly face going inside. I took out my sleeping bag, took off my coat, and slept in my car with the doors locked. The next day, I went out and bought light bulbs. I put them in every available outlet in the servants' quarters and that second night, I slept with all of them on."

In June, the founding members of *Shakespeare & Company* moved in with Krausnick to help clear the debris still covering the floors of The Mount. Some came to share his suspicion that the mansion was haunted. Some claimed to have encountered ghosts. In addition to the core of master teachers, there were two English actress friends of Packer, Gillian Bargh and Lorna Heilbron; some former NYU students including Gregory Cole and Tony Simotes; several students and faculty members from Smith and Hampshire College, including English director Kenny McBain who had been doing a workshop at Smith, and Kiki Smith, chairperson of the college's drama department. All of them had agreed to live at The Mount, sleep on floor mattresses in unfurnished rooms, share two bathrooms and one kitchen, sweep, plaster, paint, scrub, garden, and clean windows before getting around to doing any Shakespeare. For their efforts, they would all be paid a wage of $50 per week.

After a brief encounter with a local sanitation inspector who had all of them evicted while the plumbing was upgraded (the plumbing remains one of *Shakespeare & Company*'s most difficult problems), Tina Packer had to negotiate with American Actors Equity, which had to convene a special meeting to consider the problem of two British actresses performing in the Berkshires. That meeting could not be scheduled until after the summer and the two actresses were subsequently designated visiting artists at Smith College. She did not know such things as her actors' social security numbers, or anything about the American tax system. The company needed to do so many things so quickly that they had to move on several fronts at once. Their days began before six and ended long into the night. They packed into them work on the house, work on Shakespeare, and work on establishing their presence in the community.

It was clear to Packer and Krausnick that they needed to establish themselves instantly, so that they would be able to draw the 1978 Berkshire summer tourists who had already begun to crowd the local inns and cottages. They decided that the most practical way of establishing their presence and getting some attention would be to put on a free performance of *The Learned Ladies* which Packer had directed at Smith. Friends put them in touch with Beatrice Straight, a prominent American actress and Berkshire resident. She agreed to send out invitations to influential Berkshirites, inviting them to be the first to see an exciting new theater company. The *Berkshire Eagle,* in the first of what would be dozens of articles, published a small feature on the group, thereby giving them the publicity they could not have afforded otherwise.

That first performance in the small theater Packer had rejected was a stop-gap measure. Packer was determined to

72

mount a Shakespeare play that summer but the conditions in the house and the absence of theater facilities were obstacles that even she was forced to acknowledge. The company set about trying to find a natural location in which to perform. There could be no stage that summer: there was neither money nor time to construct one. Instead, the actors roamed about the grounds calling out to each other until they found a clearing in a hollow at the edge of the woods which had the best acoustics. Their choice held: one year later they built a stage on the same site.

As for a production, Packer decided to do *A Midsummer Night's Dream* for several reasons. Director Kenny McBain had just done the play at Smith; it was one of Shakespeare's most accessible and popular plays; and she liked it. Some of the Smith cast members could retain their roles, costumes could be re-used. So could props and lights. The audience would sit on the grass on an incline above the clearing in the

Packer directing her first play at The Mount

A Midsummer Night's Dream

woods that could hold a capacity audience of 450 people. Bill Ballou, one of the students, lit the stage area from the tops of evergreen trees. They decided to charge five dollars per ticket and to call it a "contribution." Rehearsals began and, in ten days, *Shakespeare & Company* made its debut in the Berkshires.

"Sheer, roistering energy is the hallmark of Shakespeare & Company's production," wrote the *Berkshire Eagle*'s critic on July 24, 1978. "There was not a pallid, pedantic moment during the entire evening. . . . Without meaning to slight the good, and in some cases, downright marvelous, acting, the behind-the-scenes stars of the show were the tumbling and fight master, B. H. Barry, and the director of movement, John Broome." The *Berkshire Courier* critic, an Englishwoman, raved: "A new company has started up in our midst and they provided me last Saturday evening with the best theatrical experience I have had in a very long time, maybe ever . . . The whole production was a feast for the eyes, ears and mind. Credit for this must be laid at the feet of Tina Packer, who has directed her company to present Shakespeare as the Bard himself would probably have wished. It is a production for the people. Nothing high and mighty and classical about it. Down to earth and yet very, very classy . . . Grab a blanket, grab a friend and get on over to the Mount. But don't delay. It is only being performed for the next two week-ends, but maybe, with luck, they'll bring it back again and again. We need more evenings like this one."

Shakespeare & Company announced that it would extend its run to August 26, about the same time that its neighbor, the Boston Symphony Orchestra, completed its season. Berkshire residents, who tend to read their local papers cover to cover, responded to the reviews and came to The Mount in sizable numbers. Summer visitors, many of whom live in

76

New York City or Boston year-round, brought weekend guests. On August 28, New York's *Village Voice* ran a short review of the production, the first in what would prove to be a thoughtful, supportive and positive set by Terry Curtis Fox. He wrote: "In the past 10 years I've seen three great *Midsummers:* John Hancock's, in which Hippolyta was played as a black slave and in which the Mendelssohn blared from a jukebox stage-right; Tim Meyer's, in which Susan Channing played Puck dressed in a riding costume; and, of course, Peter Brook's white magic show.

"Packer's production is like none of these. It is astonishingly and forthrightly 19th century. Packer has chosen the play not for its modern, passionately arbitrary sexuality, but rather for its bucolic splendor. She has played the play as pastoral—lines are basically declaimed, Bottom's transfiguration is a model of ass-head beauty, and Kiki Smith's quite wonderful costumes blend the characters into the setting rather than pushing them out of it."

Reviewers noted the actors' physical skills and the quality of their voices. They remarked on the magic of the setting, which seemed custom-designed for this production. None suspected that Tina Packer had made it cohere in only ten days of rehearsal and none differentiated between the performances of the two highly-trained British actresses and the rest of the company. Kristin Linklater had arrived in the Berkshires, back from Scotland, the day after the production opened. She, Packer and Krausnick now sat down with Mitch Berenson for an "Executive Committee" meeting to decide what to do next.

It was September, 1978. The tourists had gone home, as had the summer festivals and some members of *Shakespeare & Company*. They had, by any measure, enjoyed a successful debut but were now $25,000 in debt. Tina Packer's personal grant of $5,000 was long gone as were the other grants they had received over the summer. The three of them—Packer, Krausnick and Linklater—had given up their New York City apartments and had no place to go. On August 31, the Berkshire *Courier* ran a sympathetic feature titled: SHAKESPEARE AND COMPANY—WHAT NOW? Five days later, the *Berkshire Eagle* answered that question with the headline: SHAKESPEARE WILL BUY THE MOUNT, and followed it the next day with an editorial expressing its approval.

On September 15, the company signed a contract with Donald I. Altshuler, then owner of the mansion and surrounding grounds, to buy The Mount for $200,000. Dennis Krausnick, who suddenly took on the title of Director of Restoration, told the *Eagle* that the company had raised $6,000 toward the price of the building and that it was "prepared" to borrow another $6,000 to meet the down payment of $12,000. Mitch Berenson was willing to continue to help them, as was Dick Kapp. Six actors signed on to spend the winter at The Mount despite dire warnings about electricity stoppages and bursting pipes. *Shakespeare & Company* was ready to start building a financial base.

Dick Kapp, the man who had helped Packer obtain her first foundation grant in America, was also the person who taught her about fundraising in the U.S. Over the summer, he obtained for her company a $5,000 grant from the Lane Bryant Malsin Foundation, and a $2,000 grant from the William C. Whitney Foundation. He showed Tina Packer how to prepare for interviews and how to keep from feeling personally insulted by a rejection of her project. His own experience at the Ford Foundation was invaluable: it had taught him the importance of investigating first what a foundation's constraints were, then modifying his proposals to suit those constraints. Tina Packer now set about doing that too, with the same optimism that had launched her at The Mount.

"I learned to ring up and ask for the programming officer, to write him or her and say what we were doing," she said matter-of-factly. "Then you call the following week and ask for an appointment. They tell you what kinds of things they usually fund and whether or not they're liable to fund *you*. Then you send in a formal proposal and wait to hear what they say. They may turn you down the first time, but you come back the next year. They may turn you down a second time, but you come back a third year. By then, they know you're here to stay. The key is to keep on doing it. Not to get discouraged. The key to fundraising really is long-term relationships and persistence."

Some theater directors find fundraising so energy-depleting and ego-flattening that they hire other people to do it for them at the earliest opportunity. Packer had neither the luxury nor inclination to do that. For a while, she actually liked the process. Kristin Linklater helped write proposals but asked to be excused from the face-to-face work. Dennis Krausnick already had his hands full trying to manage the company checkbook—a task for which his vows of poverty as a Jesuit had left him singularly unprepared. "Tina had more credibility in the theater world than most people, having been an actress at the Royal Shakespeare Company, having appeared on the BBC. Most Americans responded to that," he recalled. "She was a woman with a British accent talking to American male executives. She had the credentials to talk about a 'right way' of doing Shakespeare. Also, Tina has a kind of performance energy that she brings to these meetings and a way of being able to tell what would make a person feel good about giving away his money!"

Packer has often pointed out that a long procession of British theater people—some of them women—have followed her in her quest for American foundation money and that none has been as successful. She attributes her accomplishments to an iron discipline. Since 1978, she has spent at least seven months a year doing intensive fundraising, keeping the same dawn to dusk schedule she keeps when rehearsing plays. The stress of travelling and rushing to meetings all over the country has once landed her in the hospital and added a good thirty pounds to her frame. But there is no way around it, she says. "It's simply not possible to do our kind of theater without foundation support. It's too expensive to pay actors and teachers their salaries, even if they are minimal salaries. At this point, I don't either like or dislike fundraising: it is something that must be done. In the first three years we were so poor that it involved very practical problems: how am I to get there? Is there a car? What kinds of clothes can I possibly pull together to show up in? Now I fly more often. But I always did and still do enjoy talking about my work."

Back in 1978, Packer talked to the audiences who came to The Mount. She had seen the flamboyant Ellen Stewart saunter onstage before performances began at her Café La Mama in New York, chat with audiences and solicit contributions. That first summer at The Mount, Tina Packer did the same. She walked out into the clearing at the edge of the woods, thanked the audience for coming, then—quite comfortably—asked for their ideas, time as volunteers and/ or money. "If anyone here is so turned on by the performance that they can't resist stuffing dollar bills into my hand, I will take them!" theatergoers remember her saying. One night, a child psychologist from Cambridge, Massachusetts left a $2000 check with the ticket-taker after a performance. Another night, Judy Salsbury, who had reviewed the production for the *Courier,* decided to volunteer her services as a press officer. Another night, the owner of a bookstore in Pittsfield, decided that she would organize an evening of Shakespeare after the summer to introduce the company to the community.

"I just couldn't believe how good they were," Shirley Blanchard would recall later. She had been teaching Shakespeare at the local college before founding one of the five bookstores in town and was particularly impressed that her two daughters had loved the performance. "I walked out of there and told everybody I knew that they had to go. I thought the community should get to know them. I knew they were living on nothing in this house that had been boarded up for years. Here was a group that was bringing Edith Wharton's house back to life as well as doing theater. You had the sense these were people who didn't care what they ate or drank as long as they could be acting."

Blanchard was one of the many community leaders who would play a part in making *Shakespeare & Company* a viable institution. While the rich society ladies of Miss Gertrude Robinson Smith's time were becoming a rare breed, there was still plenty of family money left in the Berkshire Hills, as well as a group of highly-paid professionals—doctors, lawyers, psychiatrists and psychologists, engineers—who could be mobilized to support a theater. Tanglewood, which had relied so heavily on community support over forty years before, now brought hundreds of thousands of dollars into the local economy. It had also instilled in Berkshirites a pride in their cultural life.

Berkshire County was clearly the sort of place which would welcome Shakespeare workshops in its schools. For the members of *Shakespeare & Company,* the idea of working with students was both attractive (most of the actors were training to become voice or movement teachers as well) and practical. If they succeeded in putting together a schools program, they reasoned, they would be able to eke out a living between summers. They wrote to every teacher and school administrator they could find, then fanned out to market their idea in the neighboring towns of Lee, Stockbridge, Housatonic, Sheffield, Dalton, Pittsfield and Great Barrington. They talked to innkeepers, shopkeepers, doctors, lawyers, religious leaders—anyone who would listen and, perhaps, help fund their project. Their first success was Bill De Vote, who had seen their production of *A Midsummer Night's Dream* and thought that he could reach into the "Special Events" budget at Housatonic Valley High School

82

where he taught. The high school, situated in Falls Village, Connecticut, turned over all its physical education classes to *Shakespeare & Company* for a week, during which time teenagers learned to shout Shakespearean expletives at the top of their lungs, to fight Elizabethan style, and to address the Bard in an even more active way than Tina Packer remembered doing as a child. The *Lakeville Journal,* a local paper, was quick to send a photographer to the gymnasium of Housatonic Valley High School and a double-page spread of pho-

tographs introduced the company and its actors to a broader audience.

Shakespeare & Company was careful to cultivate the good will of the many local papers within driving distance. Their actors were polite, available and articulate; Packer, Linklater and Krausnick were invariably "good copy," congenial, ready with interesting facts and anecdotes. It is possible to trace most of the group's early fundraising efforts that autumn simply by consulting the *Berkshire Eagle*.

In addition to "Shakespeare in the Schools," the company had determined to organize a series of workshops at The Mount where the master teachers would train outside actors. B. H. Barry gave a fight workshop. Kristin Linklater gave a month-long "Linklater Voice Workshop." The company charged $1,000 per participant for the first of their annual training sessions. The "Winter Workshops" not only helped maintain the company over the winter, but trained actors and teachers from all over the country in the kind of theater Linklater and Packer espoused. In March of 1979, a professional actors workshop held at The Mount drew such theater and movie stars as Peter Firth, Richard Dreyfuss, and Chris Sarandon. "I have come here because it gives me an opportunity to explore every facet of the actor's equipment," Richard Dreyfuss told the *Eagle,* "and integrate them through the astounding medium of Shakespeare's work." This group of actors also spread the word on *Shakespeare & Company.* Some of them even became financial contributors to it.

A third route taken by the company in that first bleak winter of 1978 had to do with Edith Wharton. All the actors had gone on a Wharton reading binge as soon as they started living at The Mount. Several, including Packer, Krausnick, and Gregory Cole, were convinced that they had encountered spirits from Edith Wharton's life during the long winter nights. The result was a series of Wharton afternoons and

84

B.H. Barry demonstrating fight technique

evenings at The Mount, during which company members performed works adapted from the novelist's books and correspondence—for money as well as love. They realized that their future was inextricably linked to the future of The Mount itself. The O'Neill Theater at Waterford, Connecticut, was greatly enhanced by its residence in the former home of playwright Eugene O'Neill. The grounds have been declared a national landmark. The Public Theater on Manhattan's Lafayette Street became a landmark once Joseph Papp raised half a million dollars in 1966 and persuaded the City of New York to buy what was then the Astor Library and rent it to the theater at one dollar per year.

Shakespeare & Company now turned its energies to persuading the National Trust for Restoration, a private organization chartered by Congress in 1949, to purchase The

Mount. The mansion had been declared a National Historic Landmark in 1974. Under the National Trust's endangered properties program, it was eligible for purchase by the National Trust—provided that a local organization repurchased it within three years. Eventually, two separate corporations—*Shakespeare & Company* and Edith Wharton Restoration—were formed so that if one went bankrupt, the other would not be held liable for its debts.

All these activities had their origin in the communal kitchen of The Mount where Tina Packer, Dennis Krausnick, Kristin Linklater and six other members of the company met every morning for breakfast. They were a most heterogeneous group. Gregory Uel Cole was a young black actor and former NYU student who was training to teach voice with Kristin Linklater. Andrea Haring was a blond, blue-eyed "Smithie" who had been raised in New Jersey. John Hadden had just left college at SUNY/Purchase and was in the throes of a massive rebellion against his WASP parents in Maine. Linklater's son, Hamish, was then a toddler. Packer's son, Jason, was 13.

"We were all *so different*," members of that first group exclaimed later when recollecting the winter. Some of the company members fell passionately (and hopelessly) in love with the others. Some were in the process of "finding themselves"; others had had it and were taking a break from the process. Some ensconced themselves in the old mansion; Natsuko Ohama, a Japanese-Canadian actress commuted between the National Arts Center in Ottawa and Lenox. They did almost everything together, dividing up the household duties into "areas of consciousness" such as "Kitchen," "Hallway," "Library," "Bathroom," working on movement and voice training, and, like so many other people shut into their homes during winters in New England, they drove each other crazy.

86

Packer as Edith Wharton, Krausnick as Henry James

Their first General Manager, Bill Liberman, had driven away in his red sports car at the end of the summer. Accustomed to managing theaters for the Shubert Organization on Broadway, he had no patience with communal living and the peculiar items that had to be figured into the company's budget such as yards of chicken-wire to fence in the garden. And, as Packer later put it, "It's very difficult to be a managing director when you're heavily in debt and there's no money to manage. Bill was the first of seven managing directors."

As the winter dragged on, the plumbing and heat broke down and so did the group's morale. Some were convinced that the spirit of Edith Wharton's unhappy marriage was hovering over them all. Kristin Linklater was more down to earth. "Creating a company is always a heartbreaking process," she said. "It hardly ever works: there's always blood

on the floor before the third or fourth production. By the fourth month in that house, we were all ready to kill one another. I had seen the gory nature of what happens when a group trains together and the leader becomes a father or mother figure. The children turn on him or her and want to rend them from limb to limb."

Tina Packer, too, was now sensitive to the dangers of allowing group dynamics to take over. Her first *Shakespeare & Company* had been destroyed that way and the memory of her shock had been preserved not only by her friends but by such former associates as Peter Hall, who had become director of the National Theater in London.

"Comical interview with Tina Packer," Hall had noted in his diary, parts of which were published later. "She had run the company as a democracy, three or four of them had intrigued against her, and in the end she had had to sack one of them. I told her that, in my view, in twenty people you will always find two or three outright shits. And a group wants to be led. If it is not led, somebody replaces the leader. She said this was right-wing and Enoch Powell-like. I said, yes, I supposed it was, but actors didn't go to work with groups, they went to work with the people who led those groups—Joan Littlewood, Ariane Mnouchkine, Peter Brook. They wanted leaders. And if she was running a group, she was a leader. She couldn't start something and then not take responsibility for it. Leaders must be checked and abused but they are certainly necessary."

By 1978, Packer says, she had far clearer ideas about running a company than she had had five years earlier. Still, she was committed to finding an alternative to authoritarianism and one winter night, at a party, she and Kristin Linklater agreed "that in the latter half of the twentieth century, it was ridiculous not to make use of the science of groups." The man who had occasioned this conclusion was John

Wehrle, a psychologist who had trained in both England and the United States, who had recently moved to the Berkshires, and who was, like Dennis Krausnick, a former Jesuit priest. Wehrle, a slightly built man with a gentle manner, later confessed to feeling "terror" as he moderated his first company group therapy session at The Mount. The actors railed at each other about everything from perceived personal affronts to repeated failure to wash out the toilet bowl properly. They sat in the library swaddled in blankets, wearing gloves to warm their hands and layers of socks on their feet, shouting, sobbing, laughing, and arguing. Somehow, they came through that first winter stronger than they had been in the fall.

On July 3, 1979, they opened their second season with one of Packer's favorite plays *The Winter's Tale* which, as critics pointed out, is long, rarely performed, difficult, and absent from American high school and college reading lists. Again, the two British actresses arrived from London along with Kiki Smith and Bill Ballou from Northampton, and master teachers John Broome and B. H. Barry from their latest stop on the theater circuit. This time, there was long training with Kristin Linklater prior to performance and six weeks of rehearsal with Tina Packer. Halfway through the summer, the company introduced *Romeo and Juliet* directed by Dennis Krausnick and the reviews in the wake of two enormously different productions were extravagant in their praise.

Some critics familiar with the Stratford Festival productions in Ontario, Canada pointed out that Tina Packer, with a low-budget and a troupe of far less experienced actors, had produced two productions superior to those at the older, richer institution. They all noted the performers' flair for comedy, their physical prowess, their cohesion as a group. They remarked on the elegance of the company's new stage, built at the edge of the woods. Most of all, they marvelled at the clarity with which the actors delivered their lines. Tina Packer would soon tire of theatergoers rushing up to congratulate her on what she thought was a minimal accomplishment, but many people in her audience were finding that they were understanding the words Shakespeare had written for the first time in their lives. Elderly people noticed that they could hear stage whispers as well as shouts. Teenagers discovered that the words were not all that different from what they were accustomed to on TV. Although the actors were all encouraged to remain true to their native accents be they Southern or New York or Oxbridge, they were all clearly intelligible and the effect was a Shakespeare restored to mass audiences.

This was precisely Tina Packer's intention and it sparked a grass roots reaction. Contributions came in, often in the form of $20 and $50 donations, from people who had never contributed to an arts organization before. Volunteers came forward with offers to work for free. The "Shakespeare in the Schools" program that the company offered was the talk of county principals as well as pupils. But while all was well on the artistic front, *Shakespeare & Company* was, by the fall of 1979, $150,000 in debt. Six general managers came and went before a board of directors was formed. It then conducted a search for a general manager who would stay. The company dug in for another winter of workshops and fundraising and teaching at The Mount.

People familiar with the histories of other theater companies wondered how the group managed to stay together and why relatively few company members left embittered or disappointed, despite the tumultuous company therapy sessions, the austerity wages, and the terrible living conditions in the deteriorating mansion. One reason, cynics said, was that there is never an abundance of jobs for actors and that when they have an opportunity to join a group, they sacrifice to stay with it. But that did not explain the loyalty of Packer's master teachers who continued with the troupe through thick and thin nor of those young actors who, even after they were able to perform all over the country, returned to *Shakespeare & Company* whenever they could.

"For me, *Shakespeare & Company* is always a learning experience," Trish Arnold mused during one of the annual workshops. "I always leave with something new and I always feel a sense of accomplishment that is lacking in other places I have taught. When you have a core of teachers who have worked with each other for as long as we have, teaching becomes an entirely different experience. Under normal circumstances, I teach a movement class, the students leave at

91

the end of it, and I have no idea what they took with them. Here I meet with the other teachers at the end of the day for a feed-back session and someone working on voice or text will say to me: 'What did you do this morning? So-and-so came in wonderfully relaxed and able to do my work.' I can feel a real concrete sense of having achieved something."

Natsuko Ohama, the Japanese-Canadian actress who was one of the founding members of *Shakespeare & Company,* has often told other actresses that, as a woman with clearly Asiatic features, nowhere else would she have the opportunity to play leading Shakespearean roles. "Tina is my favorite director because she is not as form-directed as other directors," she said. "There are many actors for whom this is a problem. They want more of a structure than she provides. But for me, her way of working is incredible. I have a real sense of creation in every performance. Most shows you see are geared toward opening night. They're set. And then, gradually, the performances die. Our productions always seem to get better so that, by the end, we are doing our best shows instead of being glad it's over.

"The other important thing for me is that while I've been performing I've trained as a voice teacher with Kristin. Now I can support myself when I'm not performing and I get to teach with all these wonderful people. There's probably no other place in the world where all the teachers speak the same language and we all put in an enormous amount of time. I cost a fortune when I teach somewhere else. But for *Shakespeare & Company* I drive up at my own expense just to say hello."

Gregory Cole says that the primary reason he remained with the company was the opportunity to act and teach concurrently—a situation fairly common in the world of classical music where string quartets and small ensembles are often in-residence at a college or conservatory, but less frequent

92

Natsuko Ohama as Titania in 1984

in the theater world. "Acting Shakespearean texts demands larger explorations than are generally undertaken in much of the theater world," he said. "What really fascinated me was that this was a company interested in transcending stereotypes, crossing barriers, being international and multi-racial without any fuss. I like being a black actor and getting to play major roles without much ado. That just doesn't exist elsewhere. And I like the philosophy of the company, that striving for a larger experience that characterizes us."

The company's third season, the summer of 1980, was their turn-around year. Thirty-three reviewers wrote about their production of *The Tempest* and, although the *New York Times* had still not shown an interest in the troupe, Terry Curtis Fox of the *Village Voice* wrote such a rave that even New York theatergoers began to be aware of something good happening in the Berkshires.

"For the past three summers, the best theater I have seen has been at the Mount in Lenox, Massachusetts," Fox began unequivocally. "Packer's production is a model of insight, clarity, vision—well magic . . . Using Linklater's vocal technique, the actors have become so comfortable with the rhythms and structures of the verse that their speech sounds truly idiomatic, their poetic diction so direct that character and ideas emerge as if from conversation. There is no pompous breaking of meter; no pausing for Art. There are simply actors who are at home in the language, using its subtle shifts of rhythmic intensity to make the essential textual points clear . . . The notion of cross-cultural fertilization has completely taken hold. The cast of this *Tempest* ranges from conventional rep actor Harris Yulin to post-Chaikinist Arthur Strimmling, who a few years ago would never meet on the same stage. That their work could now seem as concordant as it does is testimony of the power of Packer's ideals . . . But that is what I have come to expect at *Shakespeare*

Helen Hayes at company fundraiser

& *Company*. For this theater—as free in its experimentation as it is strict in its devotion to text, as concerned with training as it is with performance, permitting such deep and textured work—is not supposed to exist anywhere, much less in the American equivalent of the greenwood. I suppose one day I'm going to have to get used to its being around. I haven't yet."

Most of the reviews were equally good. The *Hartford Courant* favorably compared Packer's accomplishments to the work on view in Stratford, Ontario, and noted that the art of the three-year-old company in Lenox left one "all the more dispirited" about what was happening at the American Shakespeare Theater in Stratford, Connecticut. Only the *Boston Globe* critic was dismissive of the work, complaining that there were two levels of acting: one "acceptable, commendable even;" the other, "unacceptable, terrible even." The critic, Kevin Kelly, allowed as "There is some charming work here, piecemeal as it is . . . Anyway, *Shakespeare &*

Company is well worth a visit, even with some questions."

With 33 newspapers carrying reviews of *The Tempest,* audiences at The Mount swelled and generated word-of-mouth publicity that, in a resort area such as the Berkshires, attracted theatergoers from distant parts of the country. One of them was Arthur Ballot, who had come up from Washington, D.C. where he headed the National Endowment for the Arts Theater Division. Ballot met with Packer after a performance and pledged his support. He subseqently called some private foundations on the company's behalf and began discussions with Packer that would, in 1982, result in a National Endowment Challenge grant for *Shakespeare & Company.* "Time has a wallet on its back," read the handsome brochure that the company put out three years later. A photograph of actress Helen Hayes accompanied her signed statement which read, in part, "Unlike other sectors of the economy, productivity in the arts cannot be increased by automation, computer technology or other labor saving means. No one has yet devised a way to minimize the human effort required to produce a Shakespeare play." The company asked for contributions toward a goal of $300,000 to match a $100,000 NEA challenge grant.

Over the next two years, Tina Packer saw her company mature. Her master teachers were asked to give workshops at the Denver Center Theater Company and at the Toronto Theatre Festival. Dennis Krausnick left for a year and a half to serve as Artistic Director of the American Stage Company in St. Petersburg, Florida. Packer and Kristin Linklater were invited by the British Arts Council to conduct a workshop in London on the training methods they had developed in America. Founding members of the company were not only appearing at theaters throughout the United States, but were getting married and having children. Tina Packer was all too aware of the pressures that this growth put on the company,

96

and of the need her actors felt to be acknowledged in a greater arena. "Any actor worth his salt wants to be seen in the center of his profession," she said, "and in America, the center of the theater world is in New York."

It irked her that despite the extravagant newspaper coverage her company had received from its inception in the local press, there had been no national coverage and, apart from the *Village Voice,* no interest from the papers in New York. However vibrant *Shakespeare & Company* was in real life, she realized, it would not exist in many people's minds until it was written up in the Sunday *New York Times.* She needed a stage in New York and, in 1982, after a performance of *Twelfth Night,* she got the promise of one.

Joseph Papp was the founder of the New York Shakespeare Festival, a director, and the producer of several hundred plays. Packer had met him in 1978 and had asked him for the use of one of his theaters but he had said no. She had kept in touch with him, as she did with everyone she wished to involve in her work, writing to Papp every summer when she mounted a new production, inviting him to come up to the Berkshires to see it. She had met Papp via a network she acquired through her *est* training back in 1974. At that time, she had written to Werner Erhard, founder of *est,* for permission to adapt one of the *est* exercises that impressed her for her actors. Erhard's *est* foundation became one of the first contributors to *Shakespeare & Company.* Erhard introduced her to other "esties" including the actor Raul Julia who had worked extensively with Papp.

Papp and his wife, Gail Merrifield, drove up to the Berkshires one weekend and saw *Twelfth Night.* The production, with Gregory Cole as Count Orsino and Virginia Ness as Viola, had received wonderful reviews, and Papp invited Packer to bring it to Brooklyn's Prospect Park the following year. In 1982, its fifth season, Packer's company played at

The Mount, in Brooklyn, New York, and at the American Shakespeare Theater in Stratford, Connecticut, in addition to doing Shakespeare in the Schools and the annual Winter Workshop. Packer was closer than ever to providing the year-round employment for her company that she wanted, but even this minimal level of stability had been hard-won.

Like Joseph Papp two decades earlier, Packer had managed to transform a crisis which had the potential for closing the company down into a public relations coup. In Papp's case, it had been New York City Parks Commissioner Robert Moses who, in 1959, had prohibited performance of Shakespeare in the Central Park unless Papp agreed to charge

admission. Papp refused, setting off a wave of front-page headlines that a press agent working full time could never have obtained. "MOSES CHASES SHAKESPEARE OFF PARK GRASS" and "FREE FESTIVAL DIES" and "PAPP RETURNS TO PARK" made the producer akin to a folk hero in the minds of many New Yorkers. Evenings at the Delacorte Theater became a summer tradition.

In Packer's case, the villain was not a commissioner but a piece of legislation called Proposition $2^1/_2$, voted into effect in November, 1980 in Massachusetts. One of the many copies of California's precedent-setting Proposition 13, the Massachusetts version slashed school budgets to a minimum and could have terminated the "Shakespeare in the Schools" program. Instead, community leaders stepped in to fund the program themselves and formed a Schools Committee through which they raised donations, many between $50 and $100 per year from small businesses and private citizens. By 1981, the company had played to about 10,000 public and private school pupils and college students in 75 Massachusetts, Connecticut, and New York schools. By 1984, that number had grown to 70,000 and included school children on Cape Cod as well as in the Berkshire area. Company members ran classes, taught combat, performed, and directed student productions, becoming so popular with their charges in the process that during summer productions at The Mount, their entrance onto the stage would set off cheers from teenagers in the audience.

By its seventh season, *Shakespeare & Company* had also become involved in the administrative machinery of the Massachusetts Council on the Arts, a relationship that brought Tina Packer into close contact with other theater executives in the state. She became chairperson of the Merit Aid Panel for the Massachusetts Council and a member of the Board of Overseers for the Institute for the Arts. Both positions

99

Gregory Cole as Orsino, Virginia Ness as Olivia

would seem to require more bureaucratic skills than Packer possesses but her natural sociablity helped her and both paid unexpected dividends. In addition to looking "for a foot in the door" in New York, Packer had long been interested in getting her second foot into Boston. That city, with its thousands of college students, its highly-educated population, and its surprisingly mediocre theaters, seemed a natural for *Shakespeare & Company*. But despite repeated inquiries on Packer's part, the right situation had not materialized.

Then in May of 1984, Peter Sellars, the director of The Boston Shakespeare Company, announced that he would be leaving Massachusetts to become director of the Kennedy Center's new American National Theater in Washington, D.C. One of *Shakespeare & Company*'s Board members who lived in Boston read the announcement and immediately called Packer. Packer thought for a moment, then called Dan Morley. Morley was a vice-president of the State Street Bank in Boston who, with Packer and Peter Sellars, had been serving on the Board of Overseers for the Institute for the Arts. According to Packer, their conversation lasted less than a minute.

"I hear Peter's going to Washington," she said.

"Why? Are you interested?" asked Morley.

"Yes," said Packer.

"I'll put it to them at the Board meeting," said Morley.

The Boston Shakespeare Company was a ten-year-old company which, under the direction of Bill Cain, had produced traditional productions of Shakespeare to a small, loyal audience of subscribers. Then, in the fall of 1983, young, Harvard-educated Peter Sellars took over as Artistic Director and turned the modest, somewhat predictable theater into an auspice for the avant-garde. He directed the premiere of a contemporary American opera on its stage and produced Bertolt Brecht's *Mother Courage*. Both productions attracted national attention from critics and both were guaranteed to alienate the company's subscribers. The finances of The Boston Shakespeare Company, which had been shaky even before Sellars arrived, now became problematic. The new director, who had been awarded a MacArthur Foundation "genius grant," used part of it to bail the theater out—to no avail. By the time he left for Washington, his theater was $150,000 in debt and several members of the board of directors had quit.

Packer knew only the outlines of the situation when she called Morley but the sobering details would not have stopped her. She needed a theater in Boston. Here was a Shakespeare company with a following. She acted on instinct, just as she had in acquiring The Mount exactly six years earlier. Colleagues on the state arts council recommended her for the job and, in September of 1984, she arrived in Boston as interim director of the company.

"Boston excites me for all sorts of reasons," she told the *Boston Globe*. "Not least because it's the most English of towns over here. I really fancy wandering around the streets and getting the feel of the place, becoming part of the new identity that Boston's developing. It seems clear that theater can have a key role to play in that." She acknowledged that Peter Sellars was "a terribly hard act to follow" but that her approach to theater was quite different from his. "I'm interested in long-term work, in multipronged approaches—programs in public schools and workshops and so forth—as well as exciting first-rate productions . . . I'm interested in making the investments in actors and directors, in time and energy, in the existing and potential audience that produce a real *company,* that go some way to restoring theater to a vital place in the life of the community. If I can get that kind of thing going at BoShakes, then I should think the association will go on beyond the year ahead."

On November 14, the Boston Shakespeare Company announced that Tina Packer had been appointed permanent director by the Board and that she, together with its members, had decided to cancel the 1984–1985 season. "I'm convinced that it would be deleterious in the long run to start my stint in Boston by cutting every corner and not being able to present our work in its best light," she told the *Globe*. "Peter wanted a $2 million budget for this year if he had stayed: that's unrealistic, but $1 million is reasonable. I haven't had a chance to present our case to the corporations, foundations and individual donors who can make it happen. That's what we'll be doing in the months ahead."

In a city that was, increasingly, adopting a business school vocabulary and mentality, Packer was perceived as an artist who had a solid reputation but who could also manage to keep her bookkeeping straight. The *Globe* critic who had dismissed the first production he had seen at The Mount had since warmed to the company. And Boston theatergoers, many of whom were dissatisfied with the state of theater in their city, expressed hope that Tina Packer would finally provide some of the real stuff.

Tina Packer approached her new job with customary good cheer: "Ah, you don't happen to have any children or husbands or lovers who'll become hysterical if you need to work late or travel?" was her first question of Karen Ryker, a former professor of drama whom Packer hired as her assistant. The two women and new managing director, Michael Sirota, set up shop in the damp basement of the St. Boltoph Street theater and, with a gusto that had become habitual, Packer threw herself into yet another round of fundraising. This time, however, she already had one theater almost on its feet behind her and a strong network of friends, colleagues, and private and public organizations to tap. She spent hours in airplanes and even more hours traversing the

102

state by car on the Massachusetts Turnpike. She gained weight, got sick, and talked more often about needing another "fallow" period. But for the time being, there did not seem to be one in sight.

A busy schedule lay ahead for *Shakespeare & Company*. During the summer of 1985, Packer planned to produce three Shakespearean plays at The Mount: one comedy, one tragedy, one history. These plays had to be designed so that they could play outdoors during the summer, indoors during the winter in Boston, and in a variety of settings in the 16 states the company would be touring during the rest of the year. Then there was the matter of "Shakespeare in the Schools:" the program would be brought into the Boston school system and introduced across the state. She needed to find more directors who could work with her company and keep her ever-more-complicated group of actors happy.

"You don't build a Shakespeare company without having actors doing Shakespeare nine or 10 months a year, year

after year," she told an interviewer in 1985, "and you can only sustain that at a certain level of income. In 1984 we earned 69 percent of our keep and had to raise only 31 percent. We do break even but we are absolutely busting our guts all the time. I want to increase the actors' salaries and arrange for them not to have to work so hard. Right now, they travel to get to the next place on their tour, set up in the theater, perform the same day they travel, find their motel, get to sleep, and travel again the next day. Some of them are doing this with young children along. This cannot go on indefinitely.

"But the reason *Shakespeare & Company* has worked so well in the past is because we are a team effort. I'm not devaluing my own pivotal role in that effort—it could not have happened without me—but there have been a hell of a lot of people all pushing in the same direction here and it wouldn't have happened without them either. If one person can't do something, there's always been someone else to step in for them. It's the collective spirit that has allowed us to survive. The challenge becomes: can you hang on to it?"

There are several criteria by which Tina Packer might have measured the success of *Shakespeare & Company* in the first week of 1985: respectable box office receipts, excellent reviews ("Among the best Shakespeare seen in New York in recent memory," *New York Post*, "It could not be a better introduction to Shakespeare for young audiences," *New York Times*), the number of productions mounted, and the ability to attract government and corporate support. Her company had performed well by all these standards but, as Packer looked over the scene at the Eighth Winter Workshop, the criterion that meant most to her was her company's ability to maintain a permanent group of actor/teachers.

Intimacy infused the proceedings at Wellesley College where about 55 actors and three generations of teachers had converged from all over the United States, Canada, Great Britain, and from as far away as Australia. A crew from Boston's public television station WGBH had filmed the workshop while reporters, visiting actors and directors dropped in on classes. Yet the feeling was that of a large bustling family at work on a project of utmost importance.

The workshop participants ranged in age from 20 to older

than 60, and almost all had paid $2,200 for four weeks of training and room and board in a Wellesley College dormitory. Some were students of Kristin Linklater or one of the teachers she had trained. Some had seen *Shakespeare & Company* perform on tour and wanted to learn how to do what they had seen done on stage. Still others were there at the urging of friends who had taken the workshop in previous years.

The letter each had received one month earlier from The Mount warned that the workshop would be "arduous." By the end of the first week, both the trainees and the trainers looked exhausted. Every night after dinner, they arrived at the evening lecture bundled up in layers of sweat clothes, sweaters, shawls and leggings, equipped with packages of Kleenex along with their *Complete Works of William Shakespeare*. Some were hoarse from hours of voice work, others stiff from body work. Almost all were haggard from a lack of sleep which they attributed to the emotional tumult of jam-packed, fifteen-hour work days.

They ate breakfast at 7:30. By nine, they were at work in a movement class designed to make them aware of their physical tensions and to instill in them a sensitivity to their own impulses as well as a "delight" in moving. Trish Arnold, a pleasant, agile woman who had taught Kristin Linklater 25 years earlier in London, worked with the trainees on relaxing and aligning the body. John Broome, the dapper man who had taught Tina Packer at RADA some two decades earlier and who in 1973 had been a founding member of the company in Alcester, was at hand teaching trainees to breathe deeply and move through his exercises "with the feeling of a smile." Susan Dibble, who had studied with Broome and was married to actor John Hadden, had the trainees pair off or form groups. Her work in "theater dance" added music, words and phrases to the ingredients that bound the trainees

106

together and helped to create a sense of "safety" that *Shakespeare & Company* deemed essential for working well.

It was with that "safety" in mind that Packer had devised an exercise called "Actors and Audience," in which the trainees were divided into two groups: one onstage, one watching. One by one, each person onstage was asked to divulge four vital pieces of information: the one thing they wished no one to know about them; the one thing they wanted everyone to know about them; their name; and the part of their body they were most embarrassed by.

The exercise, which Packer had adapted from one she had performed during her *est* training, was a great leveler. As actor after actor stood up to divulge his or her secret embarrassment, those in the audience giggled, wept and empathized. Actors talked about unloving parents, their sexuality, their successes and failures in life. The experience of hearing some sixty such confessions shocked some of the trainees and energized others. For everyone, it was a profound cathartic experience and, for many, it established a bottom line of communal trust. It also provided a concrete illustration of the kind of emotional power Tina Packer was after in her theater. It introduced the trainees to the no-holds-barred psychological probing that characterizes the company's work style.

Although Packer and the other master teachers did not insist on hearing the answers to the incisive questions they put to their trainees, they did insist that the trainees "allow themselves to experience" those answers. A sense of safety, the feeling that there was a strong net available to catch them if they fell, was essential during the following weeks as the actors coped with having their favorite habits and poses—some of which they had been hiding behind for years—stripped away. Hour after hour, they worked at it. After they had loosened up their bodies, they went on to voice work with Kristin Linklater or one of the teachers she had trained.

Now forty-eight and the mother of an eight-year-old son, Linklater was somewhat less forbidding than she had been thirteen years earlier at her first meeting with Packer, but she had remained an exacting teacher. She had left New York University to work on her own and now served as a consultant to such institutions as the Stratford Festival in Canada and to such directors as Mike Nichols. She had resumed acting as well and her reputation preceded her to Wellesley. When she announced in her first class that there would be no smoking, no eating, no gum-chewing, and no sipping coffee in her presence, there was not a murmur of protest. She also ordered her trainees to give up any personal exercise routine they might have, such as calisthenics or T'ai Chi, and work only on her exercises.

"We will be undoing more than doing," she declared that first day. "All those exercises may be necessary for the dancer but they are *lethal* to the actor. What we will be doing are a series of exercises designed to fine-tune the body and to make you aware of tensions or blockages—tiny things—that you may have been unaware of before. Our basic premise is that we are all equipped at birth with voices that can express every nuance of our emotional life. But as we grow up and are socialized we put limits on those voices. What you will be doing here is releasing those restraints that you have created over the years and getting to your natural voice."

Linklater who, like all the master teachers at *Shakespeare & Company,* would, without warning, transform herself into an illustration of whatever she was discussing, suddenly became an infant who learns to transform a wail of wanting into a correct—not noisy or ugly—verbal request for attention. Then she became a small boy who learns how to stick out his chest and deepen his voice in order to seem like his

108

Kristin Linklater with son, Hamish, and Dennis Krausnick

idea of a mature man. "Your physical structure and voice are ones you developed for survival in the world," Linklater told her class. "But here we are looking at how these structures serve you as an actor. Are they serving you well? Probably not. And if they are not, you need to disorganize them!"

For the entire month of their training, workshop participants struggled to break down habits they had reinforced since childhood. They were exhorted to get out of their "heads" and into their "guts," and to pay constant attention to the depth and continuity of their breathing.

"Release the jaw!" Linklater commanded, tugging with both hands at an actor's chin or cheeks, jiggling the bones until they seemed to loosen while the musclature around them relaxed. "Release the buttocks! Can you feel what you're protecting there? Relax the muscle! Let it go soft! Be sure the breath is reaching all parts of your abdomen!"

She worked extensively with the tongue, asking her students to roll, fold, lift and lower it as they sighed, moaned, yawned, laughed and hummed, producing such a din that the voice classes at Wellesley could be located as easily as the monkey house at any zoo. The voice classes continued every day, hour after hour, in small groups and large, restoring what Linklater called "a spontaneous emotional connection" to words. After the actors were loosened up and "aligned" with their spines, they were taught the company's technique of "dropping in," which Packer and Linklater had first experimented with in Alcester in 1973 and which had become integral to their way of working.

Linklater began each day by reading aloud a Shakespearean sonnet and, to illustrate "dropping in," she chose one of her favorites.

"Sit upright. Be aware of your breathing," she instructed. "Close your eyes. Be aware of the column that is your spine. Then let the word *fall* into you: let your mouth feel it, let your middle feel it. Let it play on you. What is the word saying to you? Allow my question to hang there as I give you the words and phrases as neutrally as possible. Then speak the word as you feel it.

"*Disgrace*," she began. "When were you last in disgrace? With whom? Say it! *Disgrace!* Where does it sit in your body? *Disgrace!* Say it again! *Disgrace!*

"*When in disgrace.* What's your first word? *When!* What does it mean? *When in!* What's the second word? *With fortune.* Do you think you are a lucky person? When were you last really fortunate? *And men's eyes.* Feel how your throat has to open for *eyes!* Are men more difficult to look at than women? *And men's eyes.* Would you rather be looked at by women? *And men's eyes. I all alone.* Are you a lonely person? *all alone.* Do you feel good when you walk on the beach by yourself? *I all alone.* Does alone mean lonely to you? *Beweep*

110

my outcast state: where does the word sit in your mouth? In your body? Where do you weep? *When in disgrace with fortune and men's eyes, I, all alone, beweep my outcast state . . ."*

After more than a decade of fine-tuning their training, Tina Packer and Kristin Linklater were familiar with the inevitable mood swings and emotional exhaustion that would afflict their trainees soon after they began the workshop. Linklater had, in fact, designed a map of psychological states and posted it in a central place with an invitation to trainees to track their progress with push pins through such places as the Swamp of Sloth, the Pit of Despair, the Tunnel of Blind Endeavor, and the Mirage of True Enlightenment.

"I've been singing for two years but I never felt this resonance in my head before," one actor could be overheard saying on a given evening while another mumbled miserably, "I don't know what I'm doing here. Nothing I do seems to work."

The training aimed, as Linklater said repeatedly, at an integration of four elements: the physical, the vocal, the intellectual and the emotional. Like people trying to relearn a tennis serve or a parallel turn on skis or even the right way to make a soufflé, the actors would concentrate on one thing to the detriment of everything else they had learned and, for a while, do far worse than they had done before.

The master teachers pushed them, and commiserated. The special massage therapist who had been called in as a consultant massaged them. And the training continued with small groups devoted to fight training, text, work on individual scenes. The teachers, all of whom were also actors, varied in their teaching styles as much as in their personalities. Tony Simotes, one of the original NYU students who had acted at and cleaned up The Mount in 1978, had since been trained as a Fight Director by the British B. H. Barry, and now coached his trainees in a raucous, ebullient manner. John Hadden, another founding member of the company, was, by turns, irreverent, attentive, and distracted by the antics of his toddler son who stumbled through the corridors of Wellesley. Dennis Krausnick, who was handling the difficult role of Associate Director to the woman with whom he shared a home, had a low-key approach to his trainees. He would lean back against a piece of furniture, take a drag of his cigarette, ask questions, then make quiet suggestions. Like the rest of the men in *Shakespeare & Company,* he seemed far gentler than Packer and Linklater and some of the other women.

"Where are you with this scene?" he asked one pair of actors who, obviously dispirited, had just performed for him.

"We talked through our pelvises," said one. "Then we whispered. Then we shook. I don't know where we are anymore. I just feel this incredible pressure."

"It sounds like you've explored the scene inside out," Krausnick told them. "What I'd like to do now is to make some decisions about how you'll play it."

Krausnick had returned to *Shakespeare & Company* after serving as Artistic Director in Florida for a year and a half. Like other members of the company, who frequently took time off to pursue their own interests, he had come back refreshed. In fact, he was necessary to the continued well-being of the company in a way that was particular. Krausnick looked after Packer as well as her son Jason who was now 18 and who had, for the past six years, been living with his mother. He kept the household running while she was off on her various trips, made sure there was food in the refrigerator and clean clothing in the closets. In a company that worked like a family, he provided a role model as important in its way as Tina Packer provided in hers.

Packer herself dropped in and out of the workshop between meetings for the Boston Shakespeare Company, meetings for her company at The Mount, and meetings with people who might provide financial support for either or both. Despite a crazy schedule, she looked very much like the young woman who had turned up on Kristin Linklater's doorstep thirteen years earlier. The orange tent dress was no longer in service, but even on the days that Packer flew down to New York City, she did not remotely suggest the dress-for-success look that characterized other women on the Eastern Airlines Shuttle. She now had a proper visa: she had recently obtained a "green card" that allowed her to work without restriction in the United States. Her face was still rosy and, as Linklater had once put it, "wreathed in smiles." Her hair, now streaked with gray, still looked as though she cut it herself. Her one concession to the proprieties of fundraising were a pair of low-heeled pumps, which she would usually replace as soon as she got home with a pair of battered jogging shoes.

Tina Packer had turned 46 a few months earlier. Still, as she took charge of the workshop one evening, it was easy to imagine the teenager who liked to make faces in the bathroom mirror. "Directing is such a sedentary occupation," she told friends. "You sit there with all your emotions and tensions and have no way of letting them out, whereas an actor gets to go through the cathartic experience night after night. That's the one thing I miss about acting."

That pent-up energy was now poured into coaching the actors in her Winter Workshop, coaching that was, by all accounts, far more intense than most. Packer held on to her actors, with her hands, arms, legs, sometimes with her entire body, even wrestling one of the actresses to the floor in pursuit of a characterization. Emotionally and intellectually, too, Packer was relentless, as hard on the pairs of trainees working on their scenes as Linklater.

"Where have you just come from?" she asked each actor about his character. "With whom were you speaking? Why? Where are you now? Outside? Inside? What predicament are you in? Why? What are you going to do about it? How do we know that?"

She also answered questions, the kind of questions actors are sometimes afraid to ask for fear of seeming stupid but the kind that Packer insists be raised. "How far is Suffolk from London? How long would it take me to get from one place to the other by horse? What is outside my castle wall? What, exactly, is a 'closet' in Elizabethan times?"

Packer answered questions with the fluency of a person steeped in Elizabethan language and artifacts, and when she did not know the answer to a question, said so. Like the rest of the master teachers, she had little patience for what she called "habits of performance" and set about rooting them out with the zeal of an editor eliminating clichés from a writer's copy. "Please, don't let your forehead exhibit that 'sincere' wrinkle," she said to one actor. And, "Let's get away from the beautiful actor's voice, can we?" And, "Try not to put your hands on your hips once in this entire scene." She pointed out that one actress "leaked energy" through her small, ineffectual hand movements; another was so frightened that his voice rose to a squeak; a third was so angry that he delivered all his lines in a monochromatic roar.

Packer often began by taking the psychological measure of the actor before her and trying to get him or her to concentrate at her level of intensity.

"I can't do the last lines. I've lost it," complained one distraught Ophelia.

"I'd like to see it," Packer said evenly.

"I can't. It's awful," moaned Ophelia.

"Even if it's appalling I'd like to see it," Packer said. Then, less patiently, "You know, being an actor is often doing

114

things when you don't feel like it. In the course of your career, you may often be the wrong age, the wrong sex, the wrong color. The director may be shitty to you. You may be ill. You just *use* all of that. It's all grist for your mill."

Ophelia's Hamlet, a pleasant, courteous acting teacher, was also in trouble. "Be out of control," Packer told him. "Get yourself out of this secure world you're in all the time. Think about it: when you're at Wittenberg, you do things Ophelia doesn't even know exist. You should be utterly disgusted with yourself. Do you really want to do this? The reason I ask is that when I tell you things, you make little jokes that deflect what I'm saying. I know you understand that you're supposed to feel self-hatred. I want you to experience it."

An actor's raw material, she told actors, was his or her own self. Packer left no gates untried when trying to get a trainee to connect to a character.

"What's Friar Lawrence's life been like before Romeo and Juliet came along with their problems?" she asked an older man who had given up a successful business in plastics in order to move to New York and pursue his childhood dream of acting. "You lead this rather solitary life. You have your own cell. Your herb garden. There's somewhere in you a great desire to be committed and because you know you never will, you allow yourself to get involved vicariously."

She put a palm on the actor's stomach and asked him to close his eyes, release his jaw and speak his first line from deep inside.

"Have you ever muscled in on anyone's life yourself? How far do you think he gets involved? He's been a celibate for a long time and who knows which of those weeds he's been chewing on. Have you ever been vicariously involved in someone else's love affair yourself? How did it make you feel? Now, say the lines."

To watch Packer work with actors is nothing short of amazing. Bodies which have been wooden suddenly become supple. Readings which have been superficial become charged with meaning. It is as though Packer lights a fire within each actor and it is like watching creation.

"Actually you're both very emotionally available so instead of us working on that, I'd like to work on the text itself," she told another pair of actors, this time Hamlet and his mother Gertrude. "Let's have two chairs and you sit opposite each other and as you speak your lines, begin to observe their structure."

"Now mother, what's the matter," began Hamlet, in a fury.

"Okay," Packer interrupted, chuckling. "What have you been doing right before?"

"I've been standing there thinking: don't let me go in there and kill her," said the young man playing Hamlet.

"No. No. You've been below, the king has been praying and you've been standing behind him thinking: shall I kill him or not? Right? And then you decided no, he's praying. And then you go upstairs into your mother's closet. Do you know why she sent for you?"

"She wants to talk to me," said Hamlet.

"Is this the way you normally talk to her?"

The actor stopped to think. He had not thought about that. He tried the line in a calmer way: *"Now mother, what's the matter?"*

"Hamlet, thou hast thy father much offended," Gertrude answered him.

"Mother, you have my father much offended," said Hamlet.

"So what has just happened in the structure of the text?" Packer interrupted. "There is a mimicking of the sentence structure, right? Where does the sentence vary? In what words? How does that reflect on your character?"

116

"Hamlet," said Gertrude with a new emphasis on the name and the possessive pronoun that would follow. *"Thou hast thy father much offended."*

"Mother," mimicked Hamlet, *"You have* my *father much offended."*

"Come, come," she continued, *"you answer with an idle tongue."*

"Go, go," he replied, *"you* question *with a wicked tongue."*

"Why, how now, Hamlet!"

"What's the matter now?"

"Okay there was only one you missed. Hamlet, you should pick up on *wicked* tongue in response to her *idle* tongue. Can you see the mind of the man who's writing this?"

"Have you forgot me?" Gertude continued.

"No, by the rood not so. You are the queen, your husband's brother's wife. And—would it were not so—you are my mother."

"That's very good," Packer told them. "Just let me hear that last bit again, very clearly, so that Gertrude gets the point: he thinks she's still married to his father. And then: *would it were not so, my mother.* I don't know whether any of your children have ever told you that. Or whether you have ever told *your* parents that. But it is just about the most horrible thing you can say or hear. Has Hamlet said it before? Is it: oh God, here we go again? Or is this the first time he's behaving like this? It's an interesting acting choice, how you're going to respond to it. You could switch it every night."

Packer watched the pair run through their scene again, then turned her attention to a Kate and Hotspur where Kate was clearly a decade older than her man. Packer had heard during a teacher feedback session the evening before that the actress was uncomfortable with the age difference and used the fact to make a more general point for the group. "It's really good to acknowledge that you're not sure Hotspur would find you attractive because you're so much older than he is," Packer began bluntly. "Actually, once you're up there, you make quite an interesting couple. There's music there, don't you think? But it's really important not to waste time pretending that you're 19. You can get to 19 but you have to admit you're 40 first.

"If you're gay and you're playing a big heterosexual sex scene, it's stupid to pretend you're not gay. That doesn't create the energy and the openness that we're looking for. Instead, acknowledge that you prefer men to women. If you start aligning yourself with that, you have a possibility of expanding into your heterosexuality. If you don't allow yourself to do that, you'll be stuck pretending instead of acting. And if it's not homosexuality, it's an enormous nose that gets in the way. Or a husband who would not approve of your doing whatever it is you're doing up there. You will notice that as soon as you acknowledge something is there, it will shift. If you don't acknowledge it, you will be spending all your energy covering up and the scene will be about that."

Although Packer often struck pain or fear or panic in her provocation of the actors, serving as a catalyst for outbursts of rage or sobbing or hysterical laughter, she herself remained uninvolved in the emotions she unleashed. "It's just feeling," she said with a shrug. "You just let it pass through you." Some of her trainees felt exactly the same way. Others found that their feelings had undergone such a change during the four-week workshop that when they returned home they had difficulty adapting to the lives they had led before. Rumors of divorce and separation made their way back through the grapevine. Some participants were so grateful for the training that they became contributors to the company. Most carried what they had learned back to their own companies or schools.

Packer did not take any time out after the workshop. She

resumed her two directorships full-time, looking for money and for personnel. "The organization begins to run itself when you find the right person for a job," she said, "and that person knows far more about it than you do, so you can forget about it completely. Of course, there are occasions when I intervene. I will not have powdered milk sold at the concession stand at The Mount, for example. But, generally, I'm delighted to delegate authority."

The hardest of jobs to delegate and, paradoxically, the one that was most onerous for Packer, was the job of General Manager. After six people had tried the job and Dennis Krausnick had filled in the times in-between, the Board of *Shakespeare & Company* engaged Alan Yaffe in 1983, who put the company's books in order for the first time. He was, Packer said with relief, "an excellent administrator." But the presence of any administrator put a cramp in her style. During the first two years of the company, Packer said, she had been blissfully unaware of having to calculate the costs of the projects she wished to undertake. "I just went ahead and did what I wanted to do. It was only at the end of two years that we discovered how much we were in debt."

With the advent of a general manager, Packer now had to justify whatever projects she wished to undertake in terms of dollars and cents. For example, Yaffe was surprised to find a clinical psychologist on his payroll, and Packer had to justify the cost. The Winter Workshop, Yaffe said, was not operating at optimal benefit to the company. Packer previously encouraged company members who worked in the schools program to take the training at no cost; Yaffe ended that. He raised the tuition for trainees and limited the number of scholarships. At first, he avoided the regular therapy group meetings, but after a year of wrangling with Packer over various things, he asked for a meeting at which the administrative staff would be present.

"We started the meeting and it seemed like very tame stuff to me," Packer said later. "People struggling to define how they felt about things. I thought it was all quite good." Packer had wanted to run a writer's workshop at The Mount to explore ways in which the company's training methods could be used by writers. Her old friend and mentor, Harry Mathews, whom she had met in Paris while still a teenager, had agreed to run it. She could not, Packer conceded, point to any specific potential benefits of such a workshop to the company. It was simply something she wanted to do. Yaffe did not buy that reasoning. He would be delighted to run the workshop, he said, providing it brought in money. If not, it would have to be cancelled.

Tina Packer kept uncharacteristically quiet and Yaffe said he had the feeling she was not saying what was on her mind.

"The truth is I want to annihilate you when this sort of thing happens," she finally told him. When Yaffe got upset and said he could not work under such conditions, Packer was truly surprised. "What I said had nothing to do with him in particular," she said later. "I just wanted him to understand that any demand that I justify myself in monetary terms makes me want to kill. I was just expressing that feeling."

In the spring of 1985, Alan Yaffe was still with the company and Tina Packer was still learning to live with the constraints of accountability. She could no longer say, "I want it," and get it, as she had in 1978 when she first saw the boarded-up mansion in Lenox. On the other hand, she was now directing two institutions. *Shakespeare & Company* was, as she put it, "almost standing on its own feet." It had become as respectable a Berkshire institution as the Junior League which, every year, helped the theater: it had its own volunteer organizations, a national tour, and a schools program to which high school principals attributed everything from improved classroom attendance to higher SAT scores.

120

The Boston Shakespeare Company was on its way to ridding itself of a large debt and Packer was working daily on such questions as: whom do you ask to contribute money to pay off creditors? How do you persuade creditors to accept 10 cents on the dollar for what they are owed? How do you get talented, prestigious, committed, as well as wealthy people to sit on your board while you are doing that? And what kind of theater should Boston have?

Although people asked repeatedly whether she planned to merge her two companies, or whether she would move to New York City, Packer replied that she was quite content with Lenox and Boston as "generating centers." While she never made a secret of wanting a New York stage for her productions and had welcomed playing in Brooklyn under the auspices of Joseph Papp, Packer often remarked that she found New York "too difficult at the moment." She had no network of contacts there. She was conscious of the role that the community had played in her success and, as she looked back over the development of her career, it was clear that she had achieved by slowly building relationships.

"Although I'm very ambitious," she said, "I usually make decisions about who I choose for a role or project through existing relationships rather than going out and finding the hottest new phenomenon of the moment. When I was younger, I used to think that was dreadful. That it wasn't the right way to work. Then I read the psychologist Carol Gilligan and sighed a huge sigh of relief. I wasn't the only person in the world like this. It was a way of working that was typical of women."

Moving her theater to New York was not even on her list of priorities, she said. Her top priority, for the time being, was financial, and that meant days and weeks and months of travel and fundraising meetings. Only once during the month-long workshop did her voice falter as she described the never-ending search for corporate support. The rest of the time Packer made it seem like a challenging, although exhausting, aspect of her job. Everywhere, arts institutions were in deep financial trouble due, in part, to the federal budget cuts instituted by the Reagan Administration and to steadily rising costs of everything from the paper theater tickets were printed on to actors' salaries.

"There has got to be some way of stabilizing the institution," Packer said repeatedly. "An endowment is one way. But there has got to be some hook into the mass media. Theater has traditionally been the place to which everyone comes first to learn about acting and directing. Then they go on to make money in television or in Hollywood. It's the training ground. There has to be some way of tapping into its graduates. Look at Harvard! Look at how they've organized it! We have to find some way of tapping into the process too. Theater can't go on always being the poor relation."

In the spring of 1985, Tina Packer was telling this to people in Boston where she was working out of the damp basement offices of the Boston Shakespeare Company. Her energy seemed to be holding steady at its usual stunning level and friends said the "bewitching" way in which she divested potential donors of their money was holding steady too. Occasionally she let drop that she could use another "fallow period" at her English country cottage but that she could not afford the time out.

For many of the people who knew her or worked with her or read about her in their local newspapers, Tina Packer became something of an inspiration, a different kind of heroine in a culture where women were adopting the traditional language and male models of business as their own. Packer did not look like any other head of an institution; she did not behave like one, or talk like one; and she spent time thinking about the reasons why.

122

"Women are potentially great institution builders, I think," she mused. "It's only since the advent of birth control and small families that they're going to get a crack at it and these institutions are going to be different from the ones we've seen before. That's the challenge that faces me now. How do you create a nurturing institution? Is it possible or is it a contradiction in terms? How do you create a situation which gives you the freedom to work as an artist without having to stop your work every year or five years to do fundraising again?"

Many professional women one generation behind her, I said, had concluded that they could not make a dent in the structure of existing institutions, that many of them had be-

come discouraged, bored, cynical. How did she manage to remain so buoyantly enthusiastic about her work, I wondered. Did she ever worry about getting what she wanted and then being left with nothing else to do?

Packer answered with a burst of laughter. "I'm still far from getting what I want," she said. "In order to do what I wanted to do, I had to create a theater company. In order to do that, I used up nearly all my time and was not free to indulge in the art form itself. I'm nowhere *near* where I want to be. I still haven't found the answer to having an institution that runs properly and doing the art that I want to do.

"In one year, my son Jason will be off on his own. I expect to feel an enormous surge of energy which was not available to me before now. Who knows what will happen then?"

About the Author

Helen Epstein was born in Prague, Czechoslovakia in 1947, raised on New York City's Upper West Side, and educated at Hunter College High School. She made her journalistic debut on August 21, 1968 with an eyewitness account of the Russian Invasion of Czechoslovakia, later published in the *Jerusalem Post*. While an undergraduate at the Hebrew University, she worked as a *Post* reporter. After graduating from the Columbia School of Journalism in 1971, she became a freelance magazine writer and cultural reporter. She profiled Vladimir Horowitz, Edward Birdwell, James Galway, the Juilliard String Quartet, the Canadian National Ballet, and the New York Shakespeare Festival for *The New York Times;* Leonard Bernstein for the *Soho News;* and Meyer Schapiro for *ARTnews* (for which she won a 1984 Clarion Award). Her first book *Children of the Holocaust* has been translated into Italian and Japanese. She teaches journalism at New York University and lives with her husband in Cambridge and Hinsdale, Massachusetts.

Photo Credits

Packer Receiving Ronson Award	Keystone, London
In *The Master Builder*	Gordon Hull, Southwell
With the RSC	Jaromir Svoboda, Prague
As Dora in *David Copperfield*	BBC, London
With baby Jason	Laurie Asprey, London
John Broome	Phil H. Webber, Seattle
Kristin Linklater teaching voice	Jane Edmonds, Stratford, Ontario
Dennis Krausnick directing	Natsuko Ohama, New York
Kristin Linklater with Hamish	William S. Aron, New York
Mitch and Eleanor Berenson	Jonas Dovydenas, Lenox
A Midsummer Night's Dream	Joel Librizzi, Lenox
Shakespeare in the Schools	Sue Osthoff, Philadelphia
B.H. Barry	Mark Mitchell, *Berkshire Eagle*
Romeo and Juliet	Judy Salsbury, Lenox
Natsuko Ohama as Titania	Robert D. Lohbauer, Lee
Helen Hayes	Mark Mitchell
Gregory Cole, Virginia Ness	Sue Osthoff
The Comedy of Errors	Jane McWhorter, Sandisfield
Kristin Linklater and Hamish	Patrick Mehr, Cambridge
Packer and Linklater in 1985	Patrick Mehr, Cambridge

This book is set in Times Roman.
The paper is 70-pound Glatfelter Offset.
It was typeset by NK Graphics in Keene, N.H.
and printed by Maple-Vail in York, PA.

The cover and the pages were designed by
Sally Bindari of Designworks in Watertown, MA.

If you would like to be put on the Plunkett Lake Press mailing list, please send your name and address to: Plunkett Lake Press, 551 Franklin Street, Cambridge, MA 02139. If you would like to order an additional copy of *The Companies She Keeps,* please enclose $10.00 ($10.40 for Massachusetts residents) with your name and address to cover all (book, mail, handling and sales tax in Massachusetts) charges.